Building Dynamic Faith

Jerry Falwell

THOMAS NELSON
Since 1798

NASHVILLE DALLAS MEXICO CITY RIO DE JANEIRO BEIJING

Published in Nashville, Tennessee, by Thomas Nelson. Thomas Nelson is a trademark of Thomas Nelson, Inc.

Thomas Nelson, Inc. titles may be purchased in bulk for educational, business, fundraising, or sales promotional use. For information, please email SpecialMarkets@ThomasNelson.com.

ISBN-13: 978-0-8499-1983-1
ISBN-10: 0-8499-1983-5

Printed in the United States of America
07 08 09 10 QW 5 4 3 2 1

TABLE OF CONTENTS

Building Dynamic Faith

Dedicated to
My Grandchildren

Trey
Charles Wesley
Caroline
Paul
Jonathan, Jr.
Jessica
Natalie
Nicholas

I hope you read these stories of your grandfather
and pass them on to your children and grandchildren.
These stories of faith are my spiritual legacy to you.

Foreword

GEORGE BUSH

July 18, 2005

My friend, Jerry Falwell, has come up with a fascinating concept in this new book—a 31-day process for growing one's faith.

I have long admired Jerry's own faith which led him to build a great church, a very successful university, and, of course, a successful television ministry.

I am confident this new noncontroversial book will help us learn practical lessons to gain greater faith. Incidentally, this is an honest book, for in it Jerry Falwell deals with his own failures and doubts as well as with his victories.

I hope this book helps all readers attain greater faith and growth in that faith.

George Herbert Walker Bush
41st President of the United States
1989–93

INTRODUCTION

God Wants to Stretch Your Faith

Your life is going to be changed this month because you're going to study the greatest life-changing topic in the world, faith. Jesus said, "If you have faith as a grain of mustard seed, you shall move a mountain that is a barrier in your life, and cast it into the sea" (Ma 17:20, *My Translation*). It is my prayer this book will help you learn how your faith can move mountains!

Think of some obstacles you'd like to remove from your life; God can move them if He chooses, through your faith. So dust off those old dreams and dream again. Dream big! Read every day's devotional in the next month so you can grow a dynamic faith. These devotionals will help you develop a *life purpose,* then they'll help you develop a *life plan* so you can accomplish your *life dreams.* Get ready for God to do exploits for you. It can happen if you plan and believe God for them.

Think of the *mountain barriers* in your life that hold you back from accomplishing your dreams. You may experience a "God event" in this month, so don't miss a single day. Each day will build on the previous day, all with the purpose of developing a dynamic faith in your life. You could get a health-answer to prayer or a money-answer to prayer, or a relationship-answer to prayer.

Why one month? Because it takes time to grow anything. Giant oaks are not grown overnight, and no one becomes an overnight giant for God. Think of how long it takes a baby to learn to walk. Even after a first step, the baby will probably fall a few times.

I've found in my own life that even when I began walking by faith, I still stumbled a few times. I've had to get up and start again. So these lessons stretch over one month to give you time to learn some lessons and then apply them. And if you stumble, you'll have time to get up and start again.

While these readings take one month to complete, no one can become a person of great faith in that short of a time. So look at these devotionals as the basic training that equips soldiers for their duty. These are basic lessons in faith, and every one of them is important. They are the foundation for your lifetime of growing your faith.

I've spent a lifetime walking with God, and I'm still learning valuable lessons of faith. These daily readings include some of the first lessons God taught me about faith. When I was praying for a few hundred dollars, I was learning to trust God for millions. I want you to learn some of the lessons that God taught me.

I have started each chapter with a *faith experience* from my walk with God. I am not suggesting that I am perfect, nor am I saying that I'm the best model of faith that you can find. On the contrary, I've included my mistakes and failures. We've all stumbled on the journey of faith. But even in my failures, I've learned lessons of faith. There were great victories—building Thomas Road Baptist Church, Liberty University®, and Moral Majority—and these taught me that God answers prayer. I've included many types of illustrations to help you see how faith works.

Trusting God for Big Dreams

I've begun this book by telling some of the greatest answers to prayer in my life. These chapters are designed to develop an attitude of *faith expectancy* in you. After you begin studying faith, you should be stronger than ever, so you can move some mountains in your life.

Later, you will learn some basic skills of talking daily to God about the things in your life. Just as my faith got stronger as I trusted God for answers to prayer, so you can develop dynamic faith through daily prayer. Just as a baby must learn the basics of walking before he runs, so you must learn some basic faith skills to develop mountain-moving faith.

You'll learn certain things to develop dynamic faith. But the most important lesson is to focus on your goals. A runner must develop the attitudes, skills, and endurance to run the marathon, but learning the lessons of wrestling will not help win races. In the same way, there are many lessons to learn in the Christian life, and one of them is learning to focus on the things that will develop your faith.

You must develop your personal faith if you are to move mountains. But rather than looking at the mountain, keep your focus on God and the things only God can do. Although you'll always face obstacles, your strength comes not from dealing with obstacles, but from God's ability to move them as you pray and trust Him.

You cannot grow your faith unless you purpose to grow it. If you want something you've never had, then you must do something you've never done. You must take a leap of faith into God's provision. Your faith will grow today if you do what God has told you.

Growing Daily

Often people ask me, "How can I have faith like you?" or they request, "Teach me to have greater faith." I thought about trying to write a single book on faith, but then I had a better idea. Let me help you make the journey to dynamic faith for one month. Each day we'll talk about a different aspect of how to develop dynamic faith. As God has taught me, so you can learn the same lessons. Each day you'll see a section called "Experiencing Faith." This section includes some very practical suggestions for things you can do to develop more dynamic faith.

In the end don't compare your faith to my faith or to anyone else's faith; rather, "let us run with endurance the race that is set before us, looking unto Jesus" (He 12:1–2). Jesus is your example for faith. Let's compare everything in this book with the Word of God. In the final analysis, your life and ministry must be grounded on the authority of the Bible, because only the Word of God can grow your faith (Ro 10:17).

I haven't said everything I could say, but I've tried to include the basic things you need to know and do to develop mountain-moving faith. May God bless this book to its intended purpose.

Sincerely in Christ,
Jerry Falwell
Summer 2005

DAY 1

Searching for Faith

"If you can believe, all things are possible to him who believes."

(Mk 9:23)

Today you begin a one-month journey that can radically change your life. Every one of us wants to know God better. I do. And I know you do. So as you read each day, I'll tell you—step-by-step and day-by-day—what God did to develop my faith. It's been a life-journey for me, and if you'll follow the suggestions in "Experiencing Faith" at the end of each chapter, you'll see your faith grow more dynamic every day.

This first chapter focuses on the first great challenge to faith. I learned some foundational lessons from an apparent failure in my first faith challenge. That experience helped me triumph over my reluctance and ignorance. I think you will have similar growth experiences as your faith blossoms and grows. I've included this story first to help you overcome any reluctance you have in following God. You will probably find parallels to what God is doing in your life.

As a matter of fact, this first story contains core elements of faith that helped me plant and build the 24,000-member Thomas Road Baptist Church, plus the 21,000-student Liberty University® and the politically influential Moral Majority. I mention these not to boast, but to let you know God did it and I give all credit to Him. It is not the size of the miracle of faith that matters, but the size of our God.

1

You too can develop dynamic mountain-moving faith. We serve the same God, and He wants to do just as much for you as He's done for me and many other people of faith. So don't stand on the outside looking in. Promise yourself you'll read every chapter and do each assignment in the "Experiencing Faith" section. Plan to get from this book all that God has for you.

We all have plans and dreams. Latch on to the Lord in faith because Jesus said, "Have faith in God" (Mk 11:22). And with the greater faith you'll learn through this journey, you can move any mountain-obstacle that keeps you from fulfilling your dreams. Jesus promises, "For assuredly, I say to you, whoever says to this mountain, 'Be removed and be cast into the sea,' and does not doubt in his heart, but believes that those things he says will be done, he will have whatever he says" (v. 23). So dream big!

My First Great Test of Faith

When I was a freshman at Baptist Bible College in the fall of 1952 I began attending High Street Baptist Church, one of the early megachurches with more than two thousand people in attendance. I was lost in that big church. Pastor W. E. Dowell suggested that I volunteer to teach Sunday school in the junior department.

The junior class superintendent, Max Hawkins, took one look at me and decided I was not a good candidate. He had seen plenty of pink-cheeked Bible student volunteers begin with enthusiasm, but quit when the work became tedious. He told me outright, "I don't have much hope for you Bible student types." Hawkins explained, "You start strong and fade fast." I stood my ground, insisting I wanted a Sunday school class. "Okay, Falwell," he conceded, "you can have one 11-year-old boy. That will be your test. If you can handle one student, just maybe you can handle more." One of Hawkins' aides hung a curtain around a table and two chairs in the corner of the general assembly room; I didn't even get a classroom. I would teach there, and Hawkins would be watching in the wings.

On my first Sunday, I met Daryl, a rather shy young man with dark brown eyes, large blotchy freckles, and curly blond hair. Daryl was my first real congregation. I taught from the Bible and he listened. After two weeks, the poor kid got desperate or bored enough to bring a friend for company. The weeks crawled. Nothing happened. After six Sundays, I approached Max Hawkins to tell him I was quitting.

"Give me back the roll book then." Mr. Hawkins reached out for the book. "I didn't think you would make it. I didn't want to give you the class in the first place, but did it against my better judgment."

"No," I responded with some anger and hurt, "I'm not going to quit." I gripped the roll book and pulled it away. Hawkins just shrugged his shoulders and walked away.

I went back to the college and asked the dean of students for a key to the empty dorm room on the first floor. Each afternoon for the remainder of the year, I went and prayed from 1:00 to 5:00. There was no mattress on the bed, and I stretched my body over the springs. God broke my heart over my failure with the small Sunday school class. I realized if I was unfaithful in little things, God would never bless me in big things.

In that room I read books that motivated me to greater prayer challenges. Andrew Murray became my favorite author. I began praying for myself, and I began to pray for Daryl's salvation, the other boy, and their families.

Then I read the biography of George Mueller, the man I consider to have the greatest faith since the apostle Paul. Mueller's life taught me to think big, to tell God what I wanted, and to believe God for miracles.

These and other books challenged me to pray confidently so I could minister confidently. These books challenged me to pray for big results. When I learned to pray big, it changed my whole attitude toward serving Christ, and it gave me fruit for my ministry.

The next Saturday morning, I got the two class members, then went looking for their buddies and friends—anyone who was 11 years old. Every Saturday I cut a swath across every playground and empty lot, seeking 11-year-old boys. I did everything I could to get them to come to my Sunday school class.

Every Sunday I loaded my 1941 Plymouth with children and drove them to High Street Baptist Church. The Sunday pickup route soon outgrew my vintage Plymouth, and I organized my fellow college students who had cars to help transport children to Sunday school.

I gave a Bible to each boy in my class and showed them how to study, underline, and make notations. I told Bible stories. I read and explained Bible lessons from the Old and New Testaments. I had memorization contests, when the boys quoted the verses they had learned by heart and received prizes for their work. I found that teaching the Bible was the best way to learn it for myself.

At 11 A.M. I would march the whole class into the sanctuary so that they would hear Dr. Dowell preach the Sunday morning sermon. At the end of almost every Sunday worship service, I stepped forward with one or more boys, and I led them to pray to receive Christ at the altar, then submitted them for baptism or church membership. On weeknight visitations to their homes, I often led parents or older brothers and sisters of my 11-year-olds to faith in Christ. My class moved from the curtained corner into its own Sunday school room.

When I quit teaching at the end of my first school year at Baptist Bible College, I had fifty-six regular members, and attendance in special class activities often swelled to more than a hundred 11-year-olds. All the boys became followers of Christ, and many of their mothers, dads, and friends did also. I realized for the first time that if I would pray and work, there was unlimited potential in the service of Christ.

Steps to Finding Faith

Let me share the principle that I learned from this experience that will help you find and use faith. ***Look at your gifts, talents, and*** *longings to see God's purpose in your life.* Max Hawkins hurt me when he said, "I don't think you'll make it." I had a nonchalant attitude, and I hadn't really taken responsibility for the class. When I saw that God was working in my heart, I knew I had to succeed. When you see what God is doing in your life, it'll be the beginning of your spiritual growth. If you'll stay with the lessons of this book, you'll get dynamic faith. God can do it for you because, "He who calls you is faithful, who also will do it" (1 Th 5:24).

In that empty college dorm room I got spiritual strength from Bible study, prayer, and reading the great books of Christians. Their faith built my faith. Their trust in a great God motivated me to learn more about Him and to believe Him for the same miracles that they experienced. In the same way, I want the experiences of this book to challenge you to believe God for great things in your life.

The more you talk with God, the more you will trust Him. You can get a vision of the potential of prayer from biographies of prayer warriors, including those whose stories are told in the Bible. God uses these giants of prayer to recast your vision and rekindle your fire. When you get dreams to believe God for great things, you will begin praying for great things. Your faith will grow as God answers.

That is experiencing what the Bible teaches, "from faith to faith" (Ro 1:17). It is going from small faith to larger faith. What seem now to be gigantic answers to prayer may be small compared to the future things God has for you. Also, "from faith to faith" means going from saving faith to serving faith. It means going from trusting God for strength to get through the day to trusting Him for your family and intimate circle of friends, and then moving out to trust Him wherever He leads.

Probably you are not a pastor of a large church or connected with a large ministry. God may have placed you in a secular occupation, or given you a season as a homemaker, or given you an opportunity to minister regularly but intimately with a small group of people. The chance to mold one or two lives may seem small, but God may be preparing you to minister to more, or He may use those one or two people to reach out and touch a whole industry or an unreached country—or the world. He calls you to be faithful where He has placed you and to trust Him for the big and little tasks of that place.

Experiencing Faith

We all have some kind of faith in God, but many times our faith doesn't do anything for us. It's marvelous when faith works in your daily life. So let's start where you are and reach out to a stronger faith. What is the primary thing God is saying to you right now? What does God want you to do?

Now that you've thought about what God is telling you, write it down. I use a legal pad, but you may prefer to use a PC, a PDA, or a diary. This is the first step toward journaling, which is writing down our thoughts and prayers to God. This is like keeping a diary, but it's about God and our relationship to Him.

This is all that's included in your first assignment. *Write down what God is telling you.* You may write one sentence or a couple of pages. The length is not important, the idea is the key.

As you go through this journey, you may add more information or sharpen your idea. You may change your idea, because God may say something different to you as you continue your reading. Your idea may change, because this book may radically change your journey of faith.

But we all have to begin somewhere, so begin where you are. Write down what God is telling you now.

Suggested Reading: Mark 9:14–29

DAY 2

The Things God Uses

God draws people to Himself. Think about the things in your life that make you think about God. What about little things like a baby's laugh or the innocent question of a little girl, "Why can't we see God?" What makes you think about God?

I believe God comes to every person in many ways. Many experiences get us thinking about Him. Why does God do this? Because God loves people, and He is "not willing that any should perish but that all should come to repentance" (2 Pe 3:9). More than anything else He may want for us, He wants us to know Him.

God often uses the loss of a loved one to get us to think about the next world. My sister lost a brother-in-law in the D-Day invasion. You may have lost a child or a close friend to cancer or an accident. Smaller losses can also make us think about God. We can face losses in business, friendship losses, or sometimes just being "lost" without a purpose in life. When God is trying to get through to you, how do you respond?

This chapter focuses on the ways God reveals Himself. We will look at how God was showing Himself to me before I became a true believer. The story of your experiences will be different than mine. As you read about the things God used in my life, begin thinking about people and incidents in your life that God has used and is using.

People God Used in My Life

Many influences brought me to Christ. Surely one factor was my principal at Mountain View Elementary School, Mr. Thomas W. Finch. He was a devout man and believed that children needed to be developed spiritually alongside their physical and intellectual education. He sponsored weekly chapels where we learned hymns and quoted in unison great passages from the Scriptures, including the first and twenty-third psalms, the Beatitudes, the "Golden Rule," and Paul's definition of love in 1 Corinthians 13. Mr. Finch invited guest preachers to address his elementary children, and together we learned to pray the Lord's Prayer.

However, my real spiritual development took place at home. My mom led us in a prayer of thanksgiving before our meals. When I was a child, she prayed a bedtime prayer with me. She insisted that I go to Sunday school whether I wanted to attend or not. My grandfather was an atheist and my father was an agnostic who didn't support my mom in any of her spiritual plans. After Dad had eaten Sunday morning breakfast, he headed off to work, as he did seven days a week; then Mom loaded us into the car for the short trip to the Franklin Street Baptist Church in Lynchburg, Virginia.

One very good Sunday school teacher was Richard Logwood, the teacher of my fifth-grade Sunday school class. Ten or eleven of us gathered in little rows with our Bibles and our Sunday school quarterlies in hand.

To me, the Bible was boring, but Mr. Logwood made the Old and New Testament stories exciting. He'd take off his coat, throw it on the back of a chair, and start a story while sitting down. As excitement mounted, he would jump up and begin to pace—and as he did, the classroom came to life. Although I never accepted his invitation to give my young heart to Jesus, I was impressed by the stories that he told me from the Bible. Often I puzzled over their meaning.

As I grew older I carried an unread and unmarked Bible to Sunday school, but the minute the car was parked and everyone headed into their different classrooms, I ducked out the back door and headed south on Franklin Street to the little home of my uncle, Matthew Ferguson. Sometimes Mother found me there and, with a rather pained look at my uncle, marched me back up Franklin Street to morning worship. I stopped attending Sunday school and church altogether in my teen years. I became totally uninterested in religion and unmoved by Mom's loving if subtle attempts "to win me to the Lord." But even in those adolescent years Mom's prayers for my undeveloped spiritual life were being heard and answered in unusual ways.

Mom never preached or lectured me, but every Sunday morning she turned the radio to Charles Fuller's "Old Fashioned Revival Hour" program. He was perhaps the most popular gospel preacher on the radio in the 1940s and '50s. I awakened in the morning to the cheery gospel music of Rudy Atwood, the gospel pianist, and the Revival Hour Choir. And during breakfast while I ate my hoecakes, eggs, and ham, Charles Fuller preached and I was forced to listen.

During the summer of 1949, I was chosen to represent my high school at Boys' State, a lively experience of government-in-action for high school students held that year at Virginia Polytechnic Institute and State University. I roomed with a Church of God boy from Wise, Virginia, whose name I've forgotten but whose life had a long-range effect on me.

The first night in our dorm room he introduced himself, and in the next breath he asked me if I was saved. *Saved?* I didn't even know what he was talking about, and I felt trapped because I had to listen to him all week. I was angered by his aggressive witness.

At the welcome dance that first night, I told my date that I was rooming with a religious nut. The boy didn't dance that night; later he told me that Christians didn't dance. All week long he witnessed to me about Jesus. He read passages from the Bible and knelt at his bed to pray each evening. Somehow he turned every conversation into an opportunity to share his Christian faith. And though I didn't give him one positive response, his words made a lasting impression on me. When we said good-bye at the end of the week, he said, "I'll be praying for you." I grinned and walked away, but his words about sin and its consequences were left echoing in my brain.

How God Works in the Heart

God was at work in my heart. At times I knew it, but most of the time I ignored it. I was interested in things that fascinated high school boys. I enjoyed fast cars, girls, sports, and having fun. But God used several things to get my attention, just as I'm sure He has used several things to get you thinking about Him.

God uses people to point others to Himself. Did you notice that my mother, teachers, and the roommate at Boys' State all approached me differently, and each produced a different result? What people has God used in your life, and how has God used them?

Notice some ways that God uses people. First, *a believer's godly life* makes us think of God. That was surely true of my mother and grade school principal. Also, others' reaction to us obviously influences us! I was drawn to God because my mother didn't get mad when I cut Sunday school. But I was irritated at the boy who asked me if I was "saved." He could have pushed me from God, but didn't. What he did was make me think. Have you met people like my mother and like that boy?

Another thing that draws us to God is the *prayer of a believer.* I believe my conversion resulted from my mother's prayers, along with that high school boy at Boys' State who told me, "I'll be praying for you." I'll go so far as to say that someone has prayed for every person who has ever been converted. Has anyone prayed for you to be saved? You might be surprised to learn who has been talking to God about you.

A friend once challenged me that no one prayed for the salvation of the apostle Paul. Instantly, I remembered the prayers of Stephen. As Paul was holding the coats of those who stoned Stephen, the dying man prayed, "Lord, do not charge them with this sin" (Ac 7:60).

When God is pulling you to Himself, how do you know it is God? You know your own heart. If God is talking to your heart, you'll know it; just like I know when my wife is talking to me. And God's leading will match up with what He says in Scripture.

Sometimes God uses the irritations of life to pull us to Himself. Irritations might come from sickness, problems, or failures. When irritations come—like mosquito bites—we want to scratch. But we need to look beyond our pain to see God trying to get our attention. He uses our personal frustration or fears to talk to us. How well do you listen when God speaks to you?

Experiencing Faith

Get your pen. What is happening right now in your life? *Make a list of the things (people or events) God is using to speak to you.* This list doesn't have to be long; just include the two or three things that have your attention. Remember, this list includes the good things you like and those things that are irritating.

When you get the list made, begin thinking what these things mean to you. God may be saying one thing through one event and something different in another thing. However, God usually has one powerful message He wants to get across. Is He calling you to come closer to Him? Is He pointing out a sin? Is He telling you what to do?

Take the steps to growth. Your faith will grow as you obey the voice of God. Now that you know what God is saying to you, what will you do about it? Jot down in your journal a few things you believe God wants you to do. This may involve going to church, or reading your Bible, or beginning a regular time of prayer. While these may sound good, these are the religious things most people do. God is drawing you to Himself; He's not just drawing you to religious activities.

God is drawing you into a closer relationship with Himself. That may be salvation, or it may mean rearranging priorities, or it may mean a sense of anticipation that He is about to do something special in your life.

This book is about developing dynamic faith in your life. God may have brought several experiences into your life in the past few weeks to prepare you for this journey of faith. Listing these experiences and determining what you will do is only a first step.

Now do it! I like the action word *do.* First, listen so you can know God's call to you. "He who calls you is faithful, who also will do it" (1 Th 5:24). Next, pray about what you must do. Jesus will help you. "Whatever you ask in My name, that I will do" (Jo 14:13). Then prepare yourself to do what God is saying, as did Ezra. "For Ezra had prepared his heart to seek the Law of the Lord, and to do it" (Ezra 7:10). Finally, continue following your heart. "Whatever you do, do it heartily, as to the Lord" (Col 3:23).

Suggested Reading: 1 Timothy 3:15–17; 2 Timothy 1:5–6

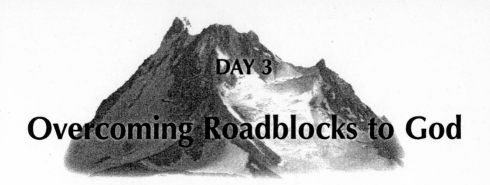

DAY 3

Overcoming Roadblocks to God

"For whoever calls on the name of the Lord shall be saved."

(Ro 10:13)

M any things can keep us from faith in Christ. For some it's a great sin in their past. My father wouldn't turn to God because he had shot and killed his brother. Some people choose the love of a family member or an illicit sexual relationship over Christ. For others, it's a little thing that they don't want to give up, like sleeping late on Sunday. For many, it's their schedule. They're just too busy for God.

What is keeping you from faith in God? It is very important to recognize the things you are putting ahead of God. Until you honestly confront your reservations, you will not be able to move forward. Take a minute to think about your roadblocks.

A Big Roadblock

My grandfather was a militant atheist. He was a hardworking man who homesteaded a farm in the Blue Ridge section of Virginia just after the Civil War. My father, Carey Falwell, was an agnostic who was described as a "bigger-than-life entrepreneur." He was a county deputy sheriff and a bootlegger at the same time. My father acquired his wealth with a multitude of businesses from a bus line to nightclubs to wholesaling and retailing gas and oil.

Perhaps the pivotal event that turned my father into an agnostic was when he shot and killed his brother Garland after a terrible argument. People said my uncle Garland was a "ne'er-do-well" and deserved it. Dad was acquitted of any wrongdoing. But just as with the first murder between brothers—Cain and Abel—my father was guilt-ridden. The guilt of that passionate moment haunted my father for the rest of his life, driving him to be an embittered alcoholic until he finally made his peace with God on his deathbed.

Dad hated hospitals and was suspicious of doctors and their mistakes. And though he was dying of the poisons in his system, he refused to be taken from our family home on Rustburg Road. Mom and my sister Virginia did their best to present the gospel to him, but he did not respond. So they sat by his bedside, watching him die and trying to make him comfortable. But the most important thing was that Mom and Virginia never gave up praying for his spiritual and physical recovery.

One afternoon in late September 1948, my sister Virginia met Frank Burford at a grocery store. Frank was a longtime business associate of my father and a friend of the family. She told him my father was "awfully sick." She invited him to visit my father and say something to him about his soul.

Frank Burford brought a huge bunch of white chrysanthemums in one hand and a basket of fresh fruit in the other. My father was not an easy man to talk to about his soul. Frank didn't know what to say or how he'd answer any question my father would ask. Frank remembers blurting out, "I want you to join the church." He felt kind of foolish as he said it.

My father answered, "I'll do it."

Frank was stunned by the sureness and suddenness of Dad's reply. Virginia and Mom looked at each other across the room, their eyes beginning to fill with tears. Frank asked, "When you gonna do it?"

"Any time you bring the man down," Dad replied. "Any time."

They both knew "the man" was a respected Presbyterian pastor in the area. So Frank drove straight over to the old Jehovah Jireh Presbyterian Church in Bocock, Virginia, to get Reverend Andrew Ponton to come explain the way of salvation to my father. Ponton had suffered a heart attack and didn't get around much.

"I'll go with you in the morning," the pastor replied. The next morning, Frank Burford had to help the old pastor into Dad's bedroom.

After my father repeated his desire to join the church, the preacher explained the plan of salvation and my father prayed to receive Christ. Pastor Ponton began, "This Sunday afternoon, we could have the elders here—"

"Don't wait till Sunday," Frank interrupted. He knew my father was very sick.

My father agreed. "I'll make my public confession of Christ right here and now."

Fifty-seven years have passed since that day my father confessed his sins and found God's forgiveness. Mom and Dad are dead. Virginia and the Reverend Ponton are dead. Frank Burford died in March 1987.

Before Burford died, he told me, "Your father just opened up and told God everything. Pretty soon he was crying. And I was crying. And Brother Ponton was crying. I didn't even try to stop my tears, because I knew the presence of the Lord was there. And when Carey prayed and asked God to forgive him, I thought my heart would break because I knew what your daddy had suffered over killing his brother. Everybody knew. And to see him get that right with God at last was something special."

My mom hurried to the kitchen, poured warm water into a bowl, and took it to the preacher. While I believe baptism is immersing a person in water, Pastor Ponton was a Presbyterian, and my father wasn't able to be baptized by immersion at that point anyway. Pastor Andrew Ponton sprinkled my father, saying, "Because you have confessed your sins and been forgiven by the Lord, as He has promised, I baptize you in the name of the Father, the Son, and the Holy Ghost. Amen."

Dealing with Roadblocks

I have outlined the roadblocks that my father faced. How does this relate to your life? Earlier I asked you to think of your own personal roadblocks. You need to address those now before you can move on. There are some principles we need to realize in dealing with barriers to faith, whether it's a roadblock in your life or in the life of someone else.

First, *identify what's keeping you from making a decision.* Maybe it's a terrible sin like that of my father. Maybe it's a series of little things that clouds your access to God. Maybe it's a habit that you can't break. Maybe you've been unconcerned and haven't realized what God is trying to do in your heart.

Don't focus on the roadblocks of life and miss seeing the road ahead, or the final destination. That's what the enemy wants you to do. He wants to get you so focused on your problems you can't see God, who is your Problem-Solver. But recognize and admit what is keeping you from God.

When you look at God, realize He is seeking you more than you—or anyone else—are looking for Him. As someone once said, "When I was looking for God, He found me."

When you look beyond the roadblocks in the road to God, you'll see His forgiveness. No matter what you have done, God will forgive you. How do I know? Because the Bible says, "The blood of Jesus Christ His Son cleanses us from all sin" (1 Jo 1:7). Did you see the phrase "all sin"? I believe God means He will forgive all sins when He says it in Scripture.

It's not what you know or how you act that makes you a Christian. When you believe in Jesus, you become a Christian. Believing in Jesus is coming to Him. Jesus said, "The one who comes to Me I will by no means cast out" (Jo 6:37). All you have to do is turn to Jesus like the thief on the cross who asked, "Lord, remember me . . ." (Lk 23:42). In response Jesus said, "Today you will be with Me in Paradise" (v. 43).

Since God offers forgiveness, you must accept it and ask Him to forgive all your sins. Since God said that forgiveness includes all sin, it's time to begin living and talking like a forgiven person. Also, since God won't change His mind, continually let this truth guide your life. Plan your life around this new relationship with God.

Now *open up to God.* Since He is calling you to Himself, and He has helped you overcome roadblocks along the way, open your heart to Him. God offers, "Call upon Me in the day of trouble" (Ps 50:15). And He promises, "The Lord is near to all who call upon Him" (Ps 145:18).

When it comes to roadblocks, *it's never too late to call on God.* The old adage says, "Where there's life, there's hope." As long as there is life, anyone can turn to God at the last minute, just as the thief on the cross dying next to Jesus received His forgiveness. But nobody is promised seventy or eighty years, so don't put it off.

God may use the most unlikely person or event(s) to reach a person. My mother was a Baptist, but she rejoiced when a Presbyterian pastor led her husband to Christ. Obviously, most of us who pray for our loved ones want to be actually involved in leading them to salvation. But the most important thing is that they get saved. Rejoice in that.

Finally, I must say something about praying for people who are away from God. **God wants us to be faithful in prayer, not just to be successful.** If you think your prayers are not successful, don't quit. If you've prayed a long time and nothing has happened, don't quit. I've been told that at the funeral of George Mueller, a long-time friend of his received the Lord for salvation. This was a person for whom Mueller prayed all his life. Mueller died without the satisfaction of seeing his friend become a Christian. But at his funeral the friend became a believer. Maybe God will not bring your loved one to Himself until after you're dead. Or maybe it'll happen but you will not know it. Nevertheless, God's main purpose for you is to be faithful in prayer.

Even though my father was hardened, my mother prayed long for him, just as she prayed long for me. I want to encourage you that if you have a family member away from God, never give up praying for the person. Pray sincerely, and pray as long as there is life in that person's body.

Experiencing Faith

Make a list. Begin listing in your journal two or three things that have kept you from God in the past. Don't make the list too extensive, or you'll lose the focus of what you are doing. List the main obstacles that blocked out God's call to you.

How were these obstacles overcome in your life? What did you do? How did God use circumstances or people to get through to you? Although belief in Jesus seems easy, we have an enemy who will use any device to keep you from listening to God's voice. So write a sentence about how the obstacles were overcome. This will build your faith and give you a basis for your future walk with God.

Now that you have listed some of the barriers to your faith, look at the following list. If one of these is your problem, study the scriptural answers. Remember, "Faith comes by hearing, and hearing by the word of God" (Ro 10:17).

Next, pray specifically about any obstacle in your life. Ask for Christ to enlighten you, give you strength to overcome the roadblock, and continue drawing you to Himself.

Help In Time of Need[1]

Can't Find Salvation	John 14:6
	Acts 16:31
	Romans 10:9
Loneliness	Psalm 23
	Isaiah 41:10
	Hebrews 13:5–6
Sorrow or Grief	2 Corinthians 1:3–5
	Romans 8:26–28

A Suffering or Trial	2 Corinthians 12:8–10
	Hebrews 12:3–13
A Time of Decision	James 1:5–6
	Proverbs 3:5–6
A Time of Danger	Psalm 91
	Psalm 121
Fear or Intimidation	Hebrews 13:5–6
	Ephesians 6:10–18
A Time of Turmoil	Isaiah 26:3–4
	Philippians 4:6–7
Time of Weariness	Matthew 11:28–29
	Psalm 23
Temptation	James 1:12–16
	1 Corinthians 10:6–13
Indifference	Galatians 5:19–21
	Hebrews 10:26–31
Forgiveness	Isaiah 1:18
	1 John 1:7–9

Suggested Reading: Mark 7:24–37

DAY 4

You Have to Make a Choice

"But as many as received Him, to them He gave the right to become children of God, to those who believe in His name."

(Jo 1:12)

Your life can be radically changed by Jesus Christ. Mine was changed on January 20, 1952. I met Jesus Christ and have never been the same since. The foundation for all I've done was built that day.

Your life can be changed just as radically as mine, because this was not about what *I* did. It's about Jesus Christ and what He has done and what He is still doing. You can develop dynamic faith to serve God just as God has taught me many lessons of trusting Him.

What's the secret to a life of faith? What's the secret to great answers to prayer? It's not about your *faith-ability*; the secret is not in you or your heart. The secret is in the *object* of your faith. That *object* is Jesus Christ.

Don't focus on the things that hold you back. And don't keep digging up past failures. Jesus Christ can change your life and help you reach your dreams. Focus on Jesus!

God has a purpose for your life, just as He has a purpose for mine. So many people go through life missing that purpose. I want this chapter to get you ready to find God's purpose and respond positively to it. God wants a relationship with you, and when you find it, everything in your life will change.

21

Conversion Changed Everything

I had no idea at the beginning of 1952 that my life would be turned inside out on January 20. The Sunday morning began uneventfully. I awakened early to the smell of hoecakes and bacon wafting up the stairs in my direction. In those days I wondered if Mom used an electric fan to blow those wonderful smells into my bedroom Sunday mornings.

For a moment I lay there breathing in my mother's love, but wishing she would let me sleep in just one Sunday morning. The radio, as always, was echoing the sermon of Charles Fuller. When I wouldn't go to church, my mother used this radio evangelist to bring the gospel to me. Finally I succumbed to the smell of fresh molasses syrup, ran down the stairs, and entered the kitchen. I was willing to listen to the sermon in exchange for a hot homemade breakfast. Mom greeted me with a good-morning hug and seated me quickly at the table. Charles Fuller was just reading his text from his radio pulpit in the Long Beach Municipal Auditorium.

I humored my mother by actually listening to Fuller's sermon that morning. I don't remember his text, but I do remember feeling something that I had never felt before. As he preached, a lump began to form in my throat. And it wasn't the hoecakes or the fatback bacon. I felt like crying, but I wasn't sad. I felt excited, but there was nothing exciting on my schedule that day. I listened to the words of the radio preacher. He asked, "Are you saved?" and I remembered the roommate at Boys' State who had asked me the very same question.

I didn't know a thing about the Holy Spirit. I didn't know what it meant to be saved or born again. But looking back, it was the presence of the Holy Spirit I was feeling. Sometimes we feel Him; other times we don't. That morning I felt Him, but didn't know what I was feeling. He was calling me, but I didn't recognize His voice. I just felt edgy and excited like the feeling before a storm strikes.

I asked my friends that afternoon, "Does anybody know a

church in Lynchburg that preaches what Dr. Fuller preaches on the radio?" A buddy answered, "Yeah, a church over on Park Avenue." He added quickly, "It's kind of a holy-roller type church, but they have good music and loads of pretty girls."

When he said, "pretty girls," I cut in with, "So, why don't we go?"

"When?" somebody asked.

"Tonight!" I answered.

Otis Wright, Jim Moon, and I drove to the 300-seat Park Avenue Baptist Church.[1] Practically every seat was full. An usher took us to the front row.

I looked down at the songbook the usher had handed me and was surprised to read *Gospel Songs from the Old Fashioned Revival Hour.* There are no coincidences when God is at work. Immediately I felt at home and believed that I had done the right thing by coming to this church.

After the sermon, the congregation began to sing, "Just as I am without one plea, O Lamb of God, I come to Thee."[2] A dozen or more young people went to the altar to pray with counselors. I felt like I was being pulled by a magnet to join them. I didn't know it was the Holy Spirit moving in my heart.

I felt embarrassed and afraid. At that moment Garland Carey, an old, white-haired gentleman standing in the pew behind me, leaned forward and whispered quietly, "Would you like me to go down there with you, son?"

"I certainly would."

Without a moment's hesitation we walked together and I knelt at that old-fashioned altar. Mr. Carey opened his Bible and led me to Christ. First, he showed me Romans 3:23, "For all have sinned and fall short of the glory of God." I acknowledged that I was a sinner; I knew I had broken God's commandments. I had taken His name in vain . . . I had lied . . . I knew I was a sinner.

Mr. Carey showed me Romans 6:23, "For the wages of sin is death, but the gift of God is eternal life." No one had to tell me I was lost and going to hell; the Holy Spirit told me. Then Mr. Carey told how Christ died for my sins—He took the punishment so I wouldn't have to go to hell.

Then Mr. Carey showed me John 1:12, "But as many as received Him, to them He gave the right to become children of God, to those who believe in His name." He asked if I would like to pray to receive Jesus into my heart. "Yes," was my simple answer.

True Belief

If you've never established a personal relationship with God, you can do it right now. I know everyone wants to know God better. I know it's your desire. So why don't you pray right now what I prayed. Salvation is as simple as praying, "Jesus, come into my heart and save me." It's as simple as praying, "Father, forgive me of my sin and receive me as Your child." It was no accident God answered my prayer. He heard me because God has promised to receive all who come to Him (Jo 6:37). So, I know God will hear and answer your prayer.

When you become a "true believer," Jesus Christ forgives your sins and gives you eternal life. A "true believer" is one who acts on what he knows about God. Trusting God for salvation is called faith. "For by grace you have been saved through faith, and that not of yourselves; it is the gift of God, not of works, lest anyone should boast" (Ep 2:8–9).

You may only be a "head believer"; you believe that there is a God, but you are not a true believer because you haven't established a personal relationship with God. Many American church members are "head believers" because they have only joined a church. They haven't established a relationship with God.

The word *believe* means we accept what we hear and act on it. We don't just know about God in our heads; we act on what we know about God. Our total personality—our intellect, emotions, and will—accepts Jesus. That means our mind, our feelings, and our will totally respond to God.

A "true believer" knows the essential facts of how Jesus became our Savior. It's knowing that Jesus suffered for us on the cross, taking our punishment, was buried, and arose from the dead on the third day. He came out of the grave to give us new life. A true believer knows these things, and knows and accepts that Jesus' death was personal—for me and you.

Next, our emotions are involved in knowing God personally. God wants you to believe with your whole self; that includes your feelings. Some people feel guilty when facing God. Others feel great love for God. They are positively motivated to seek Him. Still others are motivated by the feelings of "lostness." They feel cut off or estranged from God. Paul described these negative emotions, "I rejoice . . . that your sorrow led to repentance. . . . For godly sorrow produces repentance leading to salvation" (2 Co 7:9–10).

When you know the gospel in your head and your emotions motivate you to respond to God, you are on the road to becoming a true believer. But you must go beyond "head knowledge" and feelings. You must make a decision to ask Christ to come into your heart. This is an exercise of your will.

When I asked Jesus to come into my life, I said yes to all that I knew about God. I didn't know everything that I would later learn about God. But that night I said yes with my whole heart. Paul described this type of response, "You obeyed from the heart" (Ro 6:17). Many who are "head believers" haven't moved beyond their head knowledge of God. They haven't said yes in their hearts.

"If you confess with your mouth the Lord Jesus and believe in your heart that God has raised Him from the dead, you will be saved" (Ro 10:9). To believe with your heart is to respond with your whole inner being. To confess with your mouth is symbolic of responding with your whole outer being. Have you done so?

Experiencing Faith

Think about whether you have been converted. First you must know that you are a sinner (see Ro 3:23; 1 Jo 1:8, 10). Have you ever admitted to God you're a sinner? Notice one man's response in

Scripture, "God, be merciful to me a sinner" (Lk 18:13). If you've never done it, why don't you admit to God now that you're a sinner?

Next, you must realize Jesus died for your sin. Notice what the Bible teaches, "While we were still sinners, Christ died for us" (Ro 5:8). Stop and thank God that Jesus died for you on the cross.

But knowing Jesus died for you is not enough. You must ask Jesus to come into your life. "But as many as received Him, to them He gave the right to become children of God, to those who believe in His name" (Jo 1:12). If you've never done it, pray: "Lord Jesus, come into my life now."

Mark your prayer response to this chapter. Below is a place to check off one of three prayers. Find which applies to you and pray it now.

	Jesus, I've never done it; come into my life and make me a Christian.
	Jesus, I don't think I've done it before, even though I've been in church. Now I want You to come into my heart to make me a Christian.
	Lord, I've done it. Thank You for bringing salvation into my heart.

Suggested Reading: Luke 18:18–30

DAY 5

Developing a Dream

> "Then the Lord answered and said to me, 'Write down the vision I give to you so those on the path of life can read and understand it. The vision may be for the future, but eventually you will see the completion of the vision.'"
>
> (Hab 2:2–3, *My Translation*)

We all have dreams. Some of your dreams probably involve success at work or the happiness and success of your children. Some young people dream of succeeding at sports, or school, or in music, or something relating to their hobby or area of interest.

What about your spiritual dreams? Do you dream of living a better life or making some contribution to others? Do you want to know God better?

Am I touching a chord in your heart? Do any of your dreams relate to God? I know many people have great dreams, but they don't think deeply about God, or they won't think often about God. Even if you've only had casual thoughts about God's plans for your life, let's begin there.

Every person was put here on this earth for a reason. The reason that God put you here is really spelled out in His dream for your life. In today's reading, I tell the story of a dream for Liberty Mountain in Lynchburg, Virginia. My dream will be completely different from yours, but the principles God used to help me develop His dream in my life are the same principles that will guide you. God has a dream for your life. Find it!

We can never separate a dream from the one who has the dream. That was true of me. When God gave me a dream about a mountain, I had to do something about it. I had to put the dream on, like a person puts on a coat. Then I had to wear it daily until it became a reality.

In today's reading I want to help you discover God's dream for you, then I want you to take possession of it. I want you to wear it daily. Finding and working toward your dream will develop dynamic faith and make you a man or woman of God.

Development of a Dream

I first dreamed about the four thousand acres of Liberty Mountain when I was a boy hunting rabbits and squirrels on that mountain. I had a love for and fascination with the mountain because I lived at the eastern foot of it. Yet I didn't have any clear picture of what I wanted to do on the mountain until I began developing Liberty University® many years later.

In the early 1970s, when I was flying into the Lynchburg Municipal Airport from a preaching engagement, I looked down on Liberty Mountain upon the very spot that Liberty University® now stands. I saw these more than four thousand acres, then undeveloped. I asked a real-estate agent sitting beside me on the plane, "Who owns this property?" He told me U.S. Gypsum. Then I asked, "Is it for sale?" And he said, "Preacher, everything is for sale." I said no more. God spoke to my heart and told me, "This is the campus for Liberty University®."

After that fateful flight, I spent many days walking Liberty Mountain alone and claiming every square foot of it for the university. I claimed Joshua 1:3 as God's promise to me personally: "Every place that the sole of your foot shall tread upon, that have I given unto you" (KJV).

When I was spiritually ready, I phoned U.S. Gypsum headquarters in Chicago and made an appointment to talk with the vice president in charge of real estate. Then I flew to Chicago with the local real-estate agent. When I told the vice president I wanted to purchase the two thousand acres they owned on Liberty Mountain, he smiled and asked, "How did you know it was for sale?" He then told me about a recent board meeting where U.S. Gypsum had decided to sell off real-estate holdings around America to raise cash. It was for sale for $1,250,000.

I told the vice president my dream of building a Christian university, a camp, and massive church facilities on that mountain. He smiled in agreement with what I wanted to do. Then I asked, "Can I give you a down payment and pay it off in ninety days?" I didn't have the down payment, nor did I have any idea where the money would come from, but I believed God wanted us to have that land. Since I believed God would give us the land, I knew He'd surely give us the money to pay for it.

The vice president smiled again. He said the down payment would have to be significant. I told him I had a check for $10,000, and he began to laugh. Not a sarcastic laugh, but he just didn't believe what he was hearing. I told him I'd get $90,000 more in a few days for a total down payment of $100,000, and we'd pay it all in ninety days. Now he really laughed because he didn't think I could do it, but he agreed.

So I gave him the check for $10,000 and told him not to cash it for a few days. Now he laughed even harder, and shook his head, thinking he'd never see me again.

I don't remember where the money all came from, but we got the additional $90,000 for the down payment, and within ninety days we had the whole amount. I learned God has enough money to pay His bills when you make sure you are doing His business.

Processing Your Vision or Purpose

Let's talk about some steps that will help you process your vision or dreams. You may call it a dream that God puts in your heart. You may speak about a vision statement. (I use the word *dream* interchangeably with *vision*.) Some people just refer to what God wants them to be or do.

First, *God wants you to have dreams that are bigger than your life.* I originally had boyish dreams of Liberty Mountain, but later when I was in ministry, my dreams began to take shape. It was not a selfish dream, nor was it a dream for personal pride or personal acquisition. Liberty Mountain was a dream given to me by God.

If you work up a dream in your own energy, it may not come to pass. If it's something you want for selfish reasons, it may or may not happen. I realize many accomplish their life's dreams even though they have nothing to do with God. But when God gives you a dream, it will possess you. The dream will motivate you, and you will sacrifice your life for it.

Let me give you an action point to find your dream. *Spend time with God to get your vision from Him.* Before God gave Habakkuk a vision, the prophet said, "I will stand my watch . . . and watch to see what He [the Lord] will say to me" (Hab 2:1). The prophet had a "watch" that was a place and time where he met God. It was there that God spoke to him and gave him a dream or vision. You should have a regular time and place to meet God, so you can get His marching orders for your life. Maybe you don't know what God wants you to do in life because you haven't been meeting with Him on a regular basis and listening to what He is saying to you.

A second action point is *write down your lifelong vision.* God told the prophet Habakkuk, "Write the vision and make it plain on tablets" (Hab 2:2). Habakkuk used clay tablets to write what God told him to do; I use a legal pad. What do you use? You can write your dream on anything—your date book or journal or a PC—but the important thing is to write out your dream or vision. Why? Because writing clarifies your perspective, and writing anchors it in time. From the moment you objectify your dream in writing, you'll have a clearer idea of what God wants you to do.

Another anchor point is to *tell another your vision or life dream.* Habakkuk was told to write it down "in large, clear letters on a tablet, so that a runner can read it and tell everyone else" (Hab 2:2,

NLT). The vision was personal, but it was not private. Habakkuk was told to tell everyone about his vision. When you tell another what God wants you to do, that commits you to God's purpose. You've committed to do what your dream demands. If I had kept private my dream of Liberty Mountain, no one would have come alongside to help purchase it and develop it. I didn't have the money to purchase it, so sharing my dream was the way it became a reality. Wait for the proper time to tell someone, and don't tell someone who will be likely to shoot down your dream and tell you why it won't work.

No dream from God is strictly a personal matter. You became a Christian to serve God and help others. Life is measured in the depths of your relationship to other people, so you must share your dream with those around you. You begin by telling what God did for you in salvation, then you continue by telling others what you think God wants you to do in life.

I've been alluding to this principle all along, but now let's examine it carefully: *Your life dream gives you energy and purpose.* I'm often asked where I get my energy and drive. The answer is simple: I get it from my dream, which is God's dream for me. That's another way of saying I get my energy from God. I'm past 70 years old and won't give up, nor do I plan to retire. I have a greater dream; I have a greater energy to keep on serving until I accomplish the dream.

As believers, we all have Christ in our hearts, so His presence alone is not what drives us. Many have yielded their lives to Christ, some more than I have, so yieldedness alone is not what drives us. I believe the dream God has given me gets me up in the morning, and pushes me all day, every day. If my dream were simply a human vision, it would wear out. But since it's God's dream, I keep on going. That's why I won't quit.

Your faith is built slowly but surely on God's vision or dream. Habakkuk understood that a life vision was accomplished slowly, yet progressively. God told Habakkuk, "But these things I plan won't happen right away. Slowly, steadily, surely, the time approaches when the vision will be fulfilled. If it seems slow, wait patiently, for it will surely take place" (Hab 2:3, NLT).

I first talked about buying Liberty Mountain almost forty years ago. Then our ministry bought it. In 1977 our first buildings were constructed there. Liberty University® was located on the mountain twenty-eight years before I could relocate the Thomas Road Baptist Church to the mountain. But during those twenty-eight years, I didn't give up my faith for moving the church to the mountain. Everything has happened slowly but surely, just as our faith is developed.

Habakkuk realized he had to wait on God to fulfill the vision, but in the interim he was challenged, "The just shall live by his faith" (Hab 2:4). That's also God's challenge to you and me. We must exercise faith as we wait for our dreams to be fulfilled.

Your faith for your life's vision comes from God, and it is His faith given to you and working through you. It is His faith, His vision, His glory. Ask for His faith today so you can develop the dream God has for you. Pray as the disciples prayed, "Increase our faith" (Lk 17:5).

Experiencing Faith

Clarify your dream. Let's talk about developing your dream. First you've got to purpose to live for Christ. The more you commit your life to Christ, the more He will give you His dream for your life. And the more you surrender to Christ, the clearer your dream will become.

Maybe you can adopt the slogan, "For to me, to live is Christ" (Ph 1:21). There's no better time than now to start putting Christ first in everything. Years ago I sent out gold lapel pins that simply proclaimed "Jesus First." More than twelve million pins were distributed. Many wore that motto on their clothing. Would you wear it on your heart?

Pray. "Lord, I commit my life again to You, Jesus; I make You first in everything."

Write. Earlier I had you write what God was telling you at that time. Now I want you to take a broader perspective. Look to the past to see what God has told you previously. Do you see a dream developing in the ways God talked to you in the past? Next, look to the future. What does God want you to do in the future? Now return to today's perspective. Write now what you think God is telling you. Begin writing your dream from your present perspective.

Don't wait to write until you know everything you are to do. Sometimes writing what you know—even though it's limited—becomes a step to further insight into what God wants you to do.

Don't share your *life dream* with others just yet. First pray over what God wants you to accomplish. Reading Scripture will help focus God's dream for your life (Ma 6:31–34; Lk 9:23–26; Ro 12:1–2; Ga 2:20; Col 3:15–17, 23). In a future chapter we'll discuss sharing your dream with others.

Suggested Reading: Habakkuk 2

DAY 6

Walking by Faith

"For we walk by faith, not by sight."

(2 Co 5:7)

After you find God's dream for your life, then you must begin working to complete your dream. There's a fine line between our human initiative and God's providential work. Sometimes we must take great initiative to reach our goal. Other times we must sit back and let God work things out.

How do you know which to do? That's where faith comes in. When the Lord gives us an inner "nudge," we work as hard as we can to accomplish the dream. We push every button, turn every switch, and raise as much money as we can to get the job done. Other times the Lord inwardly holds us back, then we stop pushing and wait for the Lord to do it.

Faith is putting everything in God's hands and then letting Him tell us what to do. What's the essence of faith? It's doing what God wants us to do, not what we desire.

Paul writes, "We walk by faith, not by sight" (2 Co 5:7). In another place he tells us, "The just shall live by faith" (Ro 1:17). So how do you walk or live by faith? You must look where you're going. "Let us run with endurance . . . looking unto Jesus" (He 12:1–2). Did you see where to look? When we do something by faith, we follow Jesus' direction and do it for His glory.

God Pulls a Dream Together

God put a dream in my heart to purchase Liberty Mountain, and He allowed me to buy part of it. Then God completed the dream when our ministry purchased the largest industrial facility on the mountain. A $10.55 million miracle occurred in Lynchburg, Virginia, on February 19, 2003, when Thomas Road Baptist Church acquired the Ericsson facilities immediately next to the university campus.

The replacement cost for the mammoth Ericsson factory of 880,000 square feet and 113 acres could approach $100 million. Ericsson manufactured cell phones in this building, but the major Swedish conglomerate had made a corporate decision to quickly sell all its properties in North America. By faith, I believed God wanted us to have this property, so I prayed for God to lead me to submit the correct bid for the facilities.

Our first great answer to prayer was when Liberty's bid of $10.2 million won the right to purchase the property. I had no idea what our wonderful Lord was about to do. I never dreamed God would provide a $100-million-dollar facility to us debt-free. Without exaggeration, a modern-day miracle occurred in February 2003 when the Hobby Lobby Company, headquartered in Oklahoma City, stepped forward and provided the full $10.2 million purchase price for the Ericsson complex, plus another $350,000 to acquire the enclosed furnishings and additional acreage.

In order to fully explain what God did in this transaction, I must take you back a few weeks before we purchased the land so that you will fully understand what a marvelous thing God has done, and how He did it.

Earlier, Ericsson's attorneys had advised my son, Jerry Jr., our in-house attorney and Liberty's vice chancellor, that they wanted to close the deal with us on February 14, Valentine's Day, 2003. This meant I needed to raise $10.2 million before that date. Because of my inadequate faith, I felt that we would need more time to raise the funds. February 14 was simply too close. Our banker agreed to loan whatever amount we failed to raise by February 14 so that we could close the deal on Valentine's Day.

On the day before the closing, I flew to Oklahoma City to meet with Mr. David Green and his family, owner of the Hobby Lobby chain of about three hundred retail craft stores nationwide. He is a Christian philanthropist and is committed to spreading the gospel of Jesus Christ worldwide.

Several months earlier, Hobby Lobby had offered to donate a major property in the Greater Chicago area to Liberty University® for a branch university campus. The Chicago property housed a brand new 300,000-square-foot building on eighty acres. But the Liberty University® officials decided the Illinois facility did not fit into our long-term plans. On February 13, I flew to Oklahoma to respectfully and politely decline the Hobby Lobby gift.

While I was flying to Oklahoma City, Jerry Jr. received a communication from Ericsson saying they were postponing the closing on the Ericsson property five days, from February 14 to February 19. He called me in flight and advised me accordingly.

Now, to abbreviate a very lengthy and miraculous story, I had a three-hour, first-time-ever meeting on February 13 with David Green at the Hobby Lobby headquarters. It was in that meeting that I declined the Illinois building and told Mr. Green about the Ericsson facility in Lynchburg.

To cut to the chase, David Green said Hobby Lobby would purchase the Ericsson property and donate it to our ministries. Their attorneys and my son began five days and nights of telephone and email discussions and legal activity that resulted in Hobby Lobby closing the sale of the Ericsson property on Wednesday, February 19, with a wire of $10.55 million to Lynchburg.

The gigantic Ericsson facility, including the 113 acres, miraculously and immediately became available to us, debt-free. Praise the Lord! We paid a $1 lease fee for the first year; a year later the $10.55 million dollar building was donated to us.

It all happened so quickly and so unexpectedly! I still find myself almost stunned at what a glorious and sudden thing our Lord had done for us. We were $10.55 million ahead of where we thought we would be.

Because God provided this $10.55 million miracle, we entered the Ericsson facility debt-free. We asked permission from our donors who had already given us money to purchase Ericsson to allow us to use these funds to convert and renovate the facility. We received their unanimous permission. Obviously, we must raise several million additional dollars to thoroughly complete the conversion process over the next few years.

Learning to Walk by Faith

There are several faith principles that will keep you working toward your life's dream, even when circumstances get cloudy. Building up your faith has always been and will always be God's work. I usually write Philippians 1:6 next to my name when I autograph a Bible. That verse applies to God completing His work of salvation, but I believe it applies to every part of my life and ministry. "He who has begun a good work in you will complete it until the day of Jesus Christ" (Ph 1:6). God who began a church in a small building in Lynchburg, Virginia, carried on His work in an 880,000-square-foot factory. God who has begun to work in your heart will complete that work—if you let Him.

I believe everything we've accomplished at Thomas Road Baptist Church is the work of God. Even before I became a Christian, God put in my heart a natural love for Liberty Mountain, and that love has grown over the years. God put in me a desire to purchase the mountain long before I knew how I would use it. Never once did I believe God wanted us to have the Ericsson property at the foot of the mountain, until it came up for sale. Then God gave me a desire to buy it, and then God provided the money for it. I praise His name! Today, we own all 4,421 acres of Liberty Mountain and more than 75 buildings have been constructed.

Continually look to God to complete the dream He has put within your heart. Since it is His dream, He will complete it. I see every step that God has led me from the first building till now as His work of faith in my heart. I was looking to God and following Him, then things fell into place. Faith is "looking unto Jesus" (He 12:2) as we "run with endurance the race that is set before us" (v. 1). Faith is not looking at the mountain-obstacle, nor is it looking to the amount of money we need to purchase the mountain. Faith is just looking to Jesus.

The Lord saw the mountain long before I saw what God could do on the mountain. Our constant challenge is to see what God sees and then get our dreams in tune with God's dream. And when we get God's dream, we're exercising faith.

But you must *continually work out the dream God gives you.* Again I quote from Hebrews 12, "Since we are surrounded by so great a cloud of witnesses, let us lay aside every weight, and the sin which so easily ensnares us, and let us run with endurance the race that is set before us, looking unto Jesus" (vv. 1–2). After God shows us the dream of what He wants done—our life dream—we are responsible to get it done.

I think our responsibility involves praying for God's help, learning what it takes to reach our goal, making sacrifices, and working as hard as we can. Just as running a race involves all our physical, mental, and psychological energy, so the work of God requires everything you have. Don't hold back.

Commit to finish, by faith, what God has shown you. The verse I just quoted continues, "looking unto Jesus, the author and finisher of our faith" (He 12:2). Just as an author writes a script, so Jesus writes the message of faith in our hearts. Just as an author finishes a script, so Jesus will finish the dream. If we do our part in working diligently, God does His part to finish the project. My part was to raise money, employ staff, and motivate people to get the job done. As I did my part, the Lord did His part by touching David Green to buy the property for us. "For we are labourers together with God" (1 Co 3:9, KJV).

Faith realizes *God is in the details.* I have heard it said that "the devil is in the details," explaining why things go wrong. They say the devil will use small things to mess up something. Let's reverse the procedure. Let's say, "God is in the details," to recognize His sovereignty when things work together for good (Ro 8:28). This also recognizes that God's power is greater than Satan's attempt to destroy things. "He who is in you is greater than he who is in the world" (1 Jo 4:4).

When I look back at the acquisition of Ericsson, I see God arranging the details. Those who deal with simple home real-estate sales may have no idea how difficult it was to change the many details and change the hundreds of documents from Thomas Road Baptist Church to Hobby Lobby Company as the purchaser. Lawyers say it was a miracle to get the real-estate deal closed in five days. If we hadn't finished it in time, we would have lost our right to purchase the property. I say, "God was in the details."

Experiencing Faith

Focus. Think of all the things going on in your life. You've got family, work, church, and other responsibilities. Don't leave out your leisure activities. Of all the various activities and responsibilities, what gives you the most satisfaction? (It's not wrong to be happy doing God's plan for your life.)

Now bring all these thoughts into one focus. What does God want you to do? As soon as you get that thought—write it in your journal. Start like this: "The main thing God wants me to do is _____."

Do you realize what a fortunate person you are if you know what God wants you to do in life? Most people are going a dozen different directions at the same time. They don't have the focus that you just wrote down. They don't have a single focus in life around which they can organize the vast details that flood in on them. Happy is the person who has one purpose in life and knows how to do it.

Integrate. Spend the entire day thinking about the main thing God wants you to do. What activities help you accomplish that purpose? Make a mental list so you can write them down in your journal tomorrow when you meet God. Also, think about all the tasks you do each day that seem contrary to that purpose that you wrote down. You will want to list some of these.

Repeat often. Every time you face a task, repeat the purpose that God wants you to accomplish. Continue integrating your life around that purpose. After a couple of days, you'll have a good idea whether you're moving toward God's purpose for your life.

Focus on Jesus. Remember, as you run the race . . . look at Jesus. By thinking all day about the purpose He has for your life, you're applying faith to all your tasks. By letting the purpose of Jesus interpret your tasks, you're beginning to live by faith. Some people think faith only applies to the big things like becoming a Christian. But faith is more—it's applying Jesus' purpose for your life to all the little things you do, then doing them all for His glory.

Suggested Reading: Joshua 14:6–15

DAY 7

Getting with God

"Call to Me, and I will answer you, and show you great and mighty things, which you do not know."

(Je 33:3)

As we come to the end of our first week together, you should have gotten a new desire for greater faith. I want you to reach your dreams and move mountains by faith. In today's reading, I want you to learn the secret of developing powerful faith. As I said, I didn't intend to grow my faith, but I did intend to walk with Christ and be faithful to Him each day in my private devotions. If there's any secret to stronger faith, it's developing a stronger prayer life. Today, I want to help you develop a stronger prayer life. That's the key to reaching your dreams and overcoming obstacles in your life.

There are many ways to pray, and there are many times to pray. And so today I'll expose you to some of the many ways to pray, and we'll discuss some of the things prayer does for you.

Perhaps you have sat on the outside of God's blessing, and you can only look in to see what He does for other people. You're missing out because you have a weak prayer life. When you apply the suggestions of this chapter, you'll move closer to the heart of God, and your faith will automatically become more healthy and powerful.

Talking to God Every Day

In the first months after my conversion, my prayer life was sketchy. I ended up repeating myself or going to sleep while praying at my bedside. But I kept trying, and slowly my prayer life developed muscle. My prayer list got longer and more specific. Five minutes of meaningful prayer each day stretched to ten, and ten to fifteen minutes. As you practice prayer, may you develop the same growing sweet fellowship with God.

Not all praying is the same. The first real prayer for many is the sinner's *prayer for salvation*. But we can also converse with God through prayers of thanksgiving, prayers of surrender, prayers for forgiveness, and prayers of communion.

It was easy to give *prayers of thanks* in my beginning walk with Christ. I made lists of God's blessings and thanked Him daily for everything and everyone on the list. God had changed my life and I was deeply grateful. Suddenly I began to notice all the other wonderful gifts He had given me along the way. As I drove through Lynchburg, I thanked Him for everything good that I saw. As I met with my new friends at church, I thanked God on the spot for each of them. I hugged my mother and thanked God for her love to me.

I felt like putting my arms around the whole world and hugging it with gratitude. A verse that I had memorized in my grade school classes became real: "Enter into His gates with thanksgiving, and into His courts with praise. Be thankful to Him, and bless His name" (Ps 100:4).

Whatever your circumstances right now, whether you are rejoicing in a new promotion or mourning the recent death of a parent, God has given you many things for which you can thank Him. He loves to give good gifts to His children, and He delights in our gratitude.

Next is the daily *prayer of surrender*. When you were converted, you gave Christ everything. That is, you gave Jesus everything that you knew about. Perhaps you didn't realize new thoughts would come to your mind, along with new plans and new friends. As you encounter them, yield them all to Christ. The Christian life is one big yes to God after you receive Christ. Every day it's another yes. Pray daily what's in the Lord's Prayer, "Thy will be done."

When I pray over my events for each day, I again yield my schedule to the Lord. When I surrender each new day to the Lord, I find that I want to do His will. Then I go about planning my day because I'm yielded to Him. I recommend that you develop the habit of doing this consciously at the start of each day.

One of the first prayers many of us learn is the *prayer for forgiveness*. You need to develop the habit of confessing anything that breaks your fellowship with God. New goals you took on at your conversion may be easy to miss. Some of your old habits may be hard to break. Some of your old responses may flare automatically. Even if you have been a believer for many years, you may have begun to settle into casual patterns of living, and not always making God the center of your hourly choices. When you confess your sins and failures, God forgives you—fully.

You were forgiven when you prayed to receive Christ; don't misunderstand. God saved you from the power of sin to corrupt and kill. But Satan is still working to undermine your resolve and ruin your relationship with God. It is crucially important to deal with the sins that break your fellowship with your Father. Confess them to Him each time they pop up.

I like the bumper sticker that reads: Christians Are Not Perfect, Just Forgiven. Though the sinfulness at our core has been forgiven, you and I still fall short regularly in thought, word, and deed. We need God's forgiveness daily for the sins of commission or omission of which we are guilty.

At the end of the day, I confess to God everything that I can think of that I did, or didn't do but should have, that dishonored Him. I take my sins to the cross. I deposit them at the feet of Jesus. I ask Him to forgive them, and I leave them there knowing they are forgiven through His blood and they have no more power over me.

Then I am ready to pray and ask God for the things I need. "If we confess our sins, He is faithful and just to forgive us our sins and to cleanse us from all unrighteousness" (1 Jo 1:9).

Relational Prayers

One of the sweetest prayers develops when you learn to talk to God as a friend. When you talk to God at every available opportunity, this is the *prayer of communion*. You don't have to kneel. You don't have to close your eyes. You don't even have to start with "Dear God" and end with "In Jesus' name, Amen." This conversational style of praying can revolutionize your prayer life. It is what the Bible means by "Pray without ceasing" (1 Th 5:17). As you talk to God like you talk to a friend, little by little you will discover that He is hearing and answering your prayers.

Pray as you drive from one task to the other. Talk to God as you knock on a door or call someone on the phone, asking God to prepare the hearts of those you meet. Psalm 27:8 says it well: "When You said, 'Seek My face,' my heart said to You, 'Your face, Lord, I will seek.'"[1]

But the prayer of communion is more than just seeking God's presence; it is enjoying God and acknowledging His presence in your life. The Bible records how Nehemiah talked to God while standing before the Persian king. The king said to Nehemiah, "What do you request?" (Ne 2:4). Nehemiah didn't immediately answer the king, but "prayed to the God of heaven." He talked to God before answering the king. You can do the same thing, and pray when you face a difficult question.

A lady in the hospital asked me how she could have more faith, and I prayed before answering her. President George Herbert Walker Bush once asked me the same question. Just as Nehemiah did before the king, I prayed for God to help me answer the President. Constant prayer of communion gives meaning to the verse, "Thou art with me" (Ps 23:4, KJV).

Communion prayer teaches the truth of the abiding life. Jesus said, "I am the vine, you are the branches. He who abides in Me, and I in him, bears much fruit; for without Me you can do nothing" (Jo 15:5). The more you commune with the Lord, the easier it is to abide in Him. And that leads to God's blessing in your life, family, and ministry.

People still ask me, "How can I have faith?" I pray before I answer them. But my answer to that question is simple: The presence of Jesus in your life makes it easy to trust Him. Brother Lawrence wrote that we build our faith by "the practice of the presence of God" (see 1 Co 2:11–14). When you are constantly talking to Christ throughout the day, it's easy to grow faith and trust God for bigger things.

Perhaps the greatest lesson to learn is *prayer-worship*. When I first became a Christian, I was very action-oriented. I prayed about what I planned to do, where I planned to go, and the things in my life. Only later did I learn to spend more time in prayer, focusing on God. I had to learn what Jesus told the woman at the well, "The Father is seeking such to worship Him" (Jo 4:23). I originally spent most of my time seeking God, not realizing He was seeking worship from me.

The only thing God can't do for Himself is worship Himself. God has all the resources in the world; He doesn't need your money. However, when you properly offer your money to God, you magnify Him, which is worshipping Him. God doesn't need your service; He has all power to do anything that needs to get done. But when you properly serve Him, you exalt Him, which again is worshipping Him.

As I grew in the Lord, I spent more and more time in prayer focusing on God, and less and less time focusing on my needs and my list. So, now I begin my prayer time with either thanksgiving or worship. When God has answered a great prayer in my life or ministry, I naturally begin my quiet time by *thanksgiving prayer*. At other times, His greatness just overwhelms me, so I begin my quiet time with worship. I often turn to the Psalms to begin my worship:

How lovely is Your tabernacle, O Lord of hosts! . . . Even the sparrow has found a home, and the swallow a nest for herself, where she may lay her young—Even Your altars, O Lord of hosts, my King and my God. Blessed are those who dwell in Your house; they will still be praising You.

(Ps 84:1, 3–4)

Experiencing Faith

First, *evaluate your prayer life* with a check (✓) on the following chart:

	Never	Once	Occasionally	Frequently	Used Today
The prayer of surrender					
The prayer of thanks					
The prayer for forgiveness					
The prayer of communion					
The prayer of worship					

Make a conscious effort today to use each kind of prayer mentioned above. As you use each type of prayer ask, "Is this comfortable?" and "Is this effective?" Write your response in your journal as you use each of the above. Did prayer come easily using this expression of prayer? If not, why not? What was most enjoyable for you? Why?

Second, *make a thanksgiving list.* To learn better the prayer of thanksgiving, make a list of people and things for which you're thankful. Begin with family members and friends. You might add a phrase to tell why you're thankful for each. Do the same thing with things and events. Don't just offer thanks for people and things that make your life easy or successful, but also think of spiritual contributions to your life. What or who makes you know God better, and what or who makes you more useful in God's service?

Then *add prayer for victory to your agenda.* As you pray daily for forgiveness, you will notice that certain weaknesses or sins keep popping up. Everyone seems to have a certain sin that trips him up, more than other sins. Note these in your journal. Ask God to give you constant victory over that weakness. Learn to pray, "Lead us not into temptation, but deliver us from evil" (Ma 6:13, KJV).

Fourth, *learn conversational prayer.* This lesson suggests a few techniques to enrich your prayer life. However, you can do all these in a mechanical way and miss the point of prayer. Prayer is talking with God; it's a relationship with God. Just as you don't try to organize your conversations with friends, so you can't program all of your conversation with God. Conversational prayer is just talking informally to God. Do it often.

Fifth, *plan structure in your prayer life* by writing down a list of things for which to pray. If you were given the opportunity to talk briefly with the President of the United States, you'd plan what you'd say to make the most of your time in his presence. Do the same with God. God is the Lord of the universe. He's far more important than the President of the United States. Plan your prayer time wisely to make the most of your scheduled time with Him.

Suggested Reading: Psalm 84:1–12

DAY 8

Growing Your Faith

> "Then He said to them all, 'If anyone desires to come after Me, let him deny himself, and take up his cross daily, and follow Me.'"
>
> (Lk 9:23)

As a young Christian, I read the biographies of great men and women of faith because I wanted to be like them. I fell in love with the Lord whom they loved. I wanted to serve the Lord whom they served.

Some people give a lot of attention to building up their faith so they can move mountains for God. Their whole emphasis seems to be on their faith, and not on God who is the object of their faith. But God doesn't expect you to put your emphasis on yourself and growing your faith. Instead you should emphasize knowing and loving Him. Then your faith will grow. Don't put the cart before the horse.

I didn't set out to build great faith to accomplish great things in ministry. My original passion was a motto I learned later in my walk with the Lord, "To know Christ and to make Him known." My relationship with Christ established my faith, and the deeper I knew Him, the stronger my faith became.

Growing in Christ

I discovered early in my spiritual journey that being born again was just the beginning. The night I was converted, I went home and turned on the small light next to my bed and began reading the Bible. That lamp shined its yellow beam long into the night. I began at Matthew and read several books in the Bible. I couldn't close the Bible and go to sleep. For the first time in my life, the Bible made sense. The words leaped off the pages of Scripture. Page after page I read. Chapter after chapter. Finally, I came to the challenge that changed my life, "If anyone desires to come after Me, let him deny himself, and take up his cross, and follow Me" (Ma 16:24).

The challenge from Jesus gripped me. Sitting by my bed with an open Bible on my lap, I surrendered everything to Jesus. He said, "Come after me," and I determined to follow Jesus, no matter what. Jesus said, "Deny yourself and take up the cross" (see Mk 10:21). I didn't know fully what that meant, but I was ready to do it. Little did I know that in the next few days I would have to deny myself and take up Jesus' cross.

Jack Dinsbeer, my youth pastor, encouraged me to head back down to the Wall Gang, the group of boys I hung out with all the time. We were called the Wall Gang because we spent our time sitting on a wall next to Fairview Drug Store. Dinsbeer told me I had to share my new faith with my old friends. I had gotten into mischief with these buddies. We hadn't intentionally broken the law, but we came close. I wasn't ready to lead them to Christ, but I could at least tell them what Christ had done in my heart.

So, I told them what happened to me at the church altar. I shared with them what God did for me and how I felt. That was the first really difficult step I took to follow Christ. I felt I was taking up Christ's cross and following Him. Most of my friends received Christ within the next few months.

Steps That Contribute to Growth

Early on I learned several principles about following Jesus that you can apply to your life. First, *a Christian's first priority is to know Christ, and the second priority is to tell others about Christ.*

You should want to follow Jesus and be like Him, but you will also desire to tell your friends and family about Christ.

Perhaps you thought you would have it made once you knew what was in the Bible. Knowing Christ is a lifelong journey. His call to "come after Me" also included learning to know Him intimately. Learning a few things about Christ is never enough; there's always more to learn.

There was a second principle I learned early. *Following Jesus is a real choice.* He said, *"If* any man come after Me." The hypothetical "if" suggests we are faced with a decision to follow Him. "If" means we can either do it or not. Some people are called Christians, but they don't follow Jesus. They don't serve the Lord, nor do they grow in Christ. They don't go to prayer meetings, nor do they witness to their friends. Truly following Jesus is all the way, and it is every day.

In the third place, I found that *our inward love for Christ influences our outward life.* Jesus said, "If you love Me, keep My commandments" (Jo 14:15). When Christ came into my heart, I experienced a deep love for Him. I couldn't learn enough about Him. Every time I learned something about Christ, it challenged me to learn more. As I learned about Jesus, a lot of things I used to do fell by the wayside. Some of the things I quit were sinful; others were just no longer important.

The fourth principle is that *we will have great energy for doing those things that are motivated by our vision and that help fulfill our life plan.* After I was saved, I showed up at the church every time the doors opened. Even when there were no church services, I wanted to be with my pastors Paul Donnelson and Jack Dinsbeer, and go with them as they served the Lord. I wanted to share Christ every time an opportunity was given me.

I didn't get involved being an usher, or working on physical tasks around the church building. It's not that I refused to do manual labor for God, but other things were my priority. A task didn't catch my attention if it didn't involve ministering to people. People say I'm very relational today; that trait was first evident when I first began serving the Lord.

However, early on I learned a fifth principle: *The life of faith is doing the things God says in His Word.* A few days after I was converted, I went down to J. P. Bell Co., a local book and office supply store in downtown Lynchburg, to purchase a Scofield Reference Bible. Because I loved the Scriptures, I got the most expensive leather-bound copy they had. I kept the Bible in my car to read it when I had a few spare moments. I'd take it into the church to talk with my youth pastor about questions I discovered in my reading.

Some people refuse to serve the Lord because they don't know what to say or they haven't had training. When I felt I couldn't speak in public, I did it anyway because I wanted to honor the Lord. Some refuse to serve because they think they're not gifted with a particular spiritual gift. I've found that if you just begin serving the Lord, He'll give you the gifts or ability to do it.

The sixth principle is to *never tell God no.* In a previous paragraph I said there were certain tasks I didn't do—but I would have, if asked. I was serving, but doing things more important to me and more in line with my gifts. So the first issue deals with your desire; do first and do most what you want to do. The second issue is availability; always do what needs to be done.

From the beginning I enjoyed serving the Lord. I did everything wholeheartedly as the Scripture commands, "But before faith came, we were kept under guard by the law, kept for the faith which would afterward be revealed" (Ga 3:23).

The final principle is *follow Jesus with all your heart.* The secret of growing in Christ is to serve Him wholeheartedly with an attitude of excitement, faithfulness, and dependability. Focus on the One you're serving. You serve "as to the Lord." When Jesus is involved in your service, it has priority over everything else.

The more you know and obey the Word of God, the more faith you will develop. I don't think I ever intentionally tried to grow my faith. I just pored over the pages of the Bible, trying to remember everything I read. Everything I found in the Bible, I honestly tried to do. The more you know and obey the Word of God, the more faith you will develop. I memorized whole chapters of the Bible. When I was young, it was easy. Now that I'm older, memorizing is much harder. So my advice to the young is to learn and memorize as much Scripture as you can when you're young.

All of these experiences were strengthening my faith. I gradually felt God was calling me into full-time Christian service. On Wednesday night in March 1952, as a handful of friends at Park Avenue Baptist sang, "Jesus, Jesus, how I trust Him," I simply surrendered my old plans and said yes to God's new plans for my life. I knew God was calling me into His service full time. I didn't know what I'd do, where I'd serve. All I knew was that I'd serve Him with all my time and with all my heart.

The very next day I filled out enrollment forms for Baptist Bible College in Springfield, Missouri. From that moment on, I planned to enter Christian ministry.

Experiencing Faith

I want you to become a man or woman of God and to know Him intimately. A by-product of knowing Christ will make you a man or woman of dynamic faith.

First, you must *love the Word of God and master its contents*. Begin a daily plan to read and learn the Bible. Read five psalms every day to know God intimately and read one chapter in the book of Proverbs every day to gain wisdom. I recommend you read the *New King James Version*. It has the dignity of the past, yet reader-friendly modern expressions. Plan to read through the Bible in one year (see appendix for a suggested reading schedule).

Second, *faithfully pray through your prayer list every day.* You will develop this list in more detail in the next chapter.

Third, *find an older Christian friend to mentor you.* My friend was Jack Dinsbeer, who is on the board of Liberty University® to this day. Go to your friend with questions and for guidance. Learn from his or her years of walking with God. Now pray daily for your mentor and get him or her to pray for you (Ma 18:19).

Fourth, *look for opportunities to share your faith with others and witness for Christ.* These are growing experiences. Again, don't put the cart before the horse. You don't share your faith to grow spiritually, but you'll grow as you serve Him.

Fifth, *begin immediately to memorize Scripture.* One of the first verses I committed to memory was Philippians 1:6, "Being confident of this very thing, that He who has begun a good work in you will complete it until the day of Jesus Christ." It's a verse I use with signing my name or an autograph. Here are some other verses you should memorize:

- Philippians 1:21
- Romans 1:16
- Galatians 2:20
- Colossians 2:6
- 1 Peter 2:2
- Luke 9:23
- Ephesians 2:8–9
- Acts 4:12

My last admonition is to *be wholehearted in all you do for Christ.* Since He has given everything for you, how can you do less?

Suggested Reading: Luke 9:23, 26, 57–62

DAY 9

Putting Your Life Plan to Work

"But you shall receive power when the Holy Spirit has come upon you; and you shall be witnesses to Me in Jerusalem, and in all Judea and Samaria, and to the end of the earth."

(Ac 1:8)

Developing our faith involves two steps. First, we must get a dream from God for our life (Day 6). We call that developing a *life purpose.* The second step is developing a daily *life plan.* That's where we put God's purpose to work.

The old saying, "Plan your work, then work your plan" applies to growing your faith or any other aspect of your Christian life. If you don't have a purpose and plan, you'll wander all over the place. There's so much good work to do, you'll be working everywhere. There's so much to learn, you'll try to learn everything.

Go back to your *life purpose.* That's the concept I asked you to think about all day on Day 6. Now, let's develop a daily *life plan* to accomplish the purpose of your life. I find the best place to develop my plans is on my knees. I've discovered that if I plan my life on my knees, everything falls into place. "On your knees, pray as though it all depends on God; leave your knees and work as though it all depends on you."[1]

Today's lesson tells how I put my *life plan* to work when I first began Thomas Road Baptist Church. Your *life plan* will probably not involve full-time Christian service. It will probably involve your Christian witness to someone at work, or it may be the way you serve someone in your family. It will include your employment, your leisure, and your church activities. Whatever your *life plan*, notice how it develops your faith and makes you a man or woman of prayer.

Putting Feet to My Life Plan

At 6 A.M. on Monday morning, July 2, 1956, I unlocked the front doors of our little church in the old Donald Duck bottling company building on Thomas Road. The congregation was one week old, but the building, as our church home, was only one day old. We had just bought it.

The auditorium was empty. The cement-block building was cold and dark. I switched on a light and stood looking at the empty rows of theater chairs that we had just purchased from the old Isis Theater on Main Street. On our first Sunday many rows of those chairs had remained empty. I was determined that in the next few weeks those empty chairs would be filled to capacity.

"Lord," I prayed, "there are hundreds of people near this little building who do not know You. Help me find them. Help me reach them. Help me get them inside this place!" Less than twenty-four hours before, our little congregation had gathered in the front rows of our makeshift church. I had promised them that in just seven days we could double our attendance with new people from the neighborhood if we really worked at it.

Promising to double the attendance may have been the first *faith statement* I made with Thomas Road Baptist Church. I believed God had led us to begin this church and that God would bless our evangelistic activities. I deeply believed we could fill that auditorium in a week.

Working to fill a church is not just an exercise in pride. I had a deep belief that people who did not know Christ as Savior were spiritually lost and that it was my responsibility to share His story with them.

From the first day of your conversion, you are called to Christian witness. Sharing your faith is at the very center of what it means to be a Christian. At the time I did not know of a better way than to share it door-to-door, person-to-person. (Your *life plan* for sharing your faith may be different.)

On Monday morning I walked up that empty aisle and knelt alone at that front row of seats near the pulpit. I was scared and excited and determined. I felt God's call to Lynchburg, my hometown, and I couldn't wait to begin. I thought, *Make a decision and make it work.*

I tacked a map of Lynchburg to a poster board and put a large black dot at the place on Thomas Road that marked our church's location. Then I placed my Bible on the map, opened it to my text for that day, and read slowly the key passage from the fifth book in the New Testament, the Acts of the Apostles: "And you shall be witnesses to Me in Jerusalem, and in all Judea and Samaria, and to the end of the earth" (Ac 1:8).

That first Monday morning in my cramped office, I drew a ten-block circle with a black felt-tipped pen on the map from our church. Those ten blocks were our Jerusalem. I then traced a second penciled circle, a much wider circle; I called it Judea. That circle included a twenty-block radius from the church. The next circle included a thirty-block radius. I called that third circle our Samaria. And the rest of Lynchburg, the surrounding counties, the state of Virginia, and the nation beyond were "the uttermost parts of the earth."

I came up with a *life plan* to visit a hundred homes a day in ever-widening circles. By nine o'clock each morning, Monday through Saturday, I left my office on Thomas Road and was heading into the neighborhood to knock on doors. I carried my Bible and a yellow legal pad for taking notes.

"I'm Jerry Falwell," I began when someone answered. "I'm the pastor of a new little church meeting up here at the bottling company building. We're starting a new church, and I'd just like to invite you to come attend our services!"

People stared at me through their screens. Housewives had

dishes they were drying in their hands or a vacuum cleaner still running in the background. Unemployed men sat on the porch eyeing me with suspicion. Older widow ladies peeked out around their chain locks and listened to my invitation. Children cried. Dogs barked. Radios and televisions blared at me.

I was young, determined, and filled with enthusiasm for the task. I didn't preach to our neighbors on their front porches or read the Bible to them over the kitchen sink. I was taking my own census, trying to discover who lived in each house around our neighborhood. I wrote down the names and ages of each person in every home on the block. I kept a list of their schools, their jobs, and their churches.

I wasn't out to steal souls from other congregations in the area. In fact, I congratulated each person who claimed active church membership and wished them and their church God's best.

"By the way," I would add before leaving, "if you ever need any spiritual help, let me give you my phone number. I'd be glad to have you call me." I left a little card with each person. It didn't have a Scripture on it or an outline of God's plan of salvation, just the phone numbers of the church and my home. I told each person that if he or she called the home number, my mom would answer and would notify me immediately. My mother acted as my answering service in those days before tape machines and electronic pagers. She saw it as her ministry and wrote down each message with care and concern.

By knocking on one hundred doors every day, six days a week, I could visit six hundred homes in a week. I really believe some set their dogs on me. Others slammed their doors or listened impassively to my appeal. But at least two or three times a day I would hear a stranger say, "Please, come in. God must have sent you here. I've been praying that someone would come."

If the only person at the home was a female, I would stand at the front door and minister to her. If two or more adults were home, I would go inside. Often I would find a sick child who needed prayer, a lonely and frightened widow who needed someone to talk with, an isolated alcoholic who wanted help to cope with addiction, a couple struggling with their marriage, a young mother recently abandoned by her unemployed husband, or various victims of physical or psychological family abuse who needed serious help in escaping their predicament. I listened to each painful story. I read from the Word of God. I prayed for God's healing or direction. I advised, I counseled, I referred, and I led many to salvation in Christ. Everyone received an invitation to attend services at Thomas Road Baptist Church.

From the beginning, we published a weekly newsletter, giving a record of the growth of the church and Sunday school. The newsletter was mailed to homes visited and those who prayed to receive Christ. I wrote articles about my dream for the congregation. And though we started with just four basic services—Sunday morning worship, Sunday school, Sunday night evangelism, and a midweek prayer session—in just a few weeks there were other events, special services, and a coming revival meeting to advertise.

Each family I visited during the week would receive our little newsletter through the mails by Saturday of that week. On Saturday afternoon each home I visited would be phoned by a lady volunteer from Thomas Road Baptist Church.

I called those three contacts with our church my "triple whammy": a personal visit, a newsletter in the mailbox, and a follow-up phone call from a volunteer. And immediately these three contacts began to produce results. That next Sunday our attendance doubled. In seven days the church began to grow. The people of Thomas Road Baptist Church began to see the little storefront building fill with new people from the neighborhood.

Putting Together a Life Plan

There are four biblical foundations to my *life plan*. Your *life plan* will be different from mine, but if we work through the process together, I think you will get a better idea of how to write one. First, I believe that *all people are lost who don't believe in Jesus Christ*. On the night I received Christ as Savior, Mr. Carey showed me the verse, "God demonstrates His own love toward us, in that while we were still sinners, Christ died for us" (Ro 5:8). I believed it then, and that motivated me to go to every home near our new church. I believed everyone needed the message of Jesus Christ. That's why I made one hundred house calls each day.

Many postmoderns don't believe that all people are lost without Jesus. Some don't believe in hell, but I believe it's a *real* place where *real* people will spend a *real* eternity. A talk show host criticized me for saying that no one goes to heaven without Jesus and that all persons who don't believe in Jesus are going to hell. I told him that Baptists who don't believe in Jesus are going to hell, Presbyterians who don't believe in Jesus are going to hell, talk show hosts who don't believe in Jesus are going to hell. Because everyone is lost without Jesus, I tried to reach everyone possible.

A second fact motivated me to aggressively put my *life plan* into action. *Because Jesus died for all, it's our obligation to reach all.* Because I loved Jesus and followed Him, I wanted to reach everyone for whom He died. Successful evangelism is based on relationship. Paul said, "We continue to witness because the love of Christ motivates us to do it" (2 Co 5:14, *My Translation*).

There's a third reason that I aggressively worked my *life plan;* it's that *Jesus commanded us in the Great Commission to witness to all.* He told us, "Go into all the world and preach the gospel to every creature" (Mk 16:15). I take God's commands literally. I believe God wanted me to do two things. He wanted me to go to every person in my "Jerusalem," and therefore I went from door to door. Second, God wanted me to share the gospel with them. I believe the Great Commission is God's marching orders for you, for me.

There's a fourth principle in my *life plan. Many may not be ready to receive Christ when you go to them, so leave the door open for future ministry.* Those who will not listen to your Christian witness should know that you care and that God loves them. Then when a crisis comes, they'll remember you came to them and they'll contact you. Even if they turn you down when you first share your faith, they ought to know that you—and your church—will be praying for them. Then when they come to the end of themselves, which means they are frustrated and don't know what to do, they'll remember you and your church. They'll call you to help them spiritually. That's why I left my phone number.

Today, I go to homes by radio and television. It's my revised *life plan*. I go to homes by mail and by the Internet. Why? So when that moment comes when someone's world falls apart, they'll phone me or my church. We constantly train hundreds to knock on doors and evangelize.

You'll go to your friends differently than I do. You'll go by a friendly conversation over coffee, or by doing something for them, or by going somewhere with them. We have different *life plans,* and we have different *life purposes.* We even "go" to people differently, but it's for the same reason and it follows the same principle—to open their hearts to God and the gospel message.

What is your *life purpose?* What principles can help you apply that purpose and develop a *life plan?*

Experiencing Faith

First go back to Day 5, the day we discussed dreams, and *review your life purpose.* Then review Day 6, the day I had you write a statement of purpose, what God wants you to do with your life. Get your purpose firmly in mind.

Today, we will develop a *life plan* to give you focus in your life. This is what gave me focus in my life. My *life plan* helped develop my faith in God. It worked; people prayed to receive Christ and the church began to grow.

Now let's **begin making a list of some practical or actual things to carry out your life plan.** I drew circles on a map to guide my daily and weekly activities. Your *life plan* will be different. In addition to writing what you'll do, write out what you want to accomplish with these specific activities.

The next action point for a *life plan* is to **begin making faith state-**

ments. Remember I made a *faith statement* to double our church attendance? That was hard to do when the church was new and few people knew about us. But that *faith statement* motivated me to action. Write down what you want God to do as a result of the actual projects you will do. Don't make your *faith statement* to others just yet. Say it to your journal. Write what you plan to do, then pray about it.

Some might think we shouldn't make a *faith statement.* But Jesus said, "If you have faith as a mustard seed, you will say to this mountain, 'Move from here to there,' and it will move" (Ma 17:20). In today's assignment, you will see your faith begin to grow as your write out your *life plan.* Then, when you identify some actual projects to carry out your *life plan,* you can make a *faith statement* of what you want God to do. Your faith will grow when you begin to see your *life plan* materialize and you see your *faith statement* come about.

Suggested Reading: Acts 1:1–11

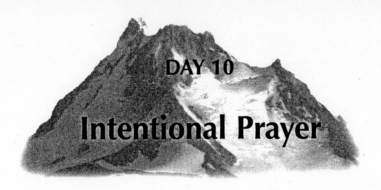

DAY 10

Intentional Prayer

> "Ask, and it will be given to you; seek, and you will find; knock, and it will be opened to you."
>
> (Ma 7:7)

W hat's it going to take to make you a great man or woman of mountain-moving faith? Vibrant faith is not built instantly. You don't just step out once in blind faith to become a person of great faith. It takes years of walking by faith to become a spiritual giant, just as it takes years for an acorn to become a towering oak. But you can be like those in the Bible whose "faith grows exceedingly" (2 Th 1:3).

One of the things that will give you dynamic faith is your daily personal time with God. This is when you talk to Him and He talks to you—friend to friend. As you establish a prayer-relationship with God, you're on your way to becoming a man or woman of God.

This chapter is about developing your prayer habits and skills so you will develop a dynamic prayer life. But to reach that level, you must have more than a regular routine of prayer. You must come to the place of enjoying prayer, and eagerly seek time to pray; so much so that you will sacrifice to pray. That will happen when you realize prayer is an ongoing relationship with God.

Planning Your Prayer Time

As a child of God, you will normally talk to God several times in each day as you go about your duties. But you also need a special time each day where you can be quiet and alone for prayer. Try to do it at the same time and place each day. Most call this their quiet time or their daily devotions.

Prayer is simply talking to God, so begin by making a list of things you want to talk to God about each day. I have a *long prayer list* and a *short prayer list* that include requests I bring before God daily.

My *long prayer list* includes each member of my family. I call each person on this list by name every day before God. I tell God the trials that each is facing and ask the Lord to help them with each specific need. My *long prayer list* includes my ministry and the ministries of others I know and love. My long list also includes my prayer partners and the people of my church. I pray for people in Lynchburg and across the country who need God's special help. I pray for my city, for the state, for the nation, and for the world. I pray for mayors, governors, senators and members of Congress, cabinet officials, and the President. I pray for the salvation of those who are lost and for God's guidance for those who love and serve Him.

You might want to add to your *long prayer list* some of the items from my list. Of course, you'll have different family, friends, and business associates. Any person, group, or organization that is on your heart or part of your relational circle should be on this list.

My *short prayer list* is constantly changing because it includes the crises or needs of the day. My short list may include asking for a certain amount of money to complete a building, or it may be for city approval for a permit. It includes people facing a health crisis and my appearances on television to speak to a national issue. Your short list won't look like mine. You'll include business and family challenges. You may include those who are sick or causing friction in your neighborhood or your church. Your short list will continually change.

Begin writing out your own prayer list. Then date it. I often write my requests on a legal pad, putting each item with others on the same topic on one page. You may use a notebook or your computer. I have a friend who keeps his prayer requests on a packet of 3x5 cards. Use whatever is most convenient for you.

Talk to God about your requests like you would talk to a friend. Return to your requests and pray for them every day until you see God's answer. Then write down the answer and its date next to each request. Writing down the answers to prayer is just as important as writing down your request. When you go back through that "diary" of answers, it will bring joy, praise, and new faith to your spiritual journey.

You can pray any place and any time. Location is irrelevant. But some places and some times are more helpful for effective, focused praying than are others. Usually, I pray in my study each morning because I'm the only one awake. I pray in the shower. Sometimes I pray in the family room. Other times I drive up Liberty Mountain and look down across the Liberty University® campus and out across the city of Lynchburg as I pray. When the mountain is quiet, I feel close to God above the noise and distractions of the city.

Everybody should have a place where praying is easy. Some people set aside a room (even an old closet) in their homes for prayer. They put in a light and a Bible, and perhaps they keep a notebook or diary or other Christian reading materials in their place of prayer. They put a sign on the door, "Prayer Closet: Do Not Disturb Except in Emergency." Friends and family know that when that door is closed, their loved one is at prayer.

Beyond having a regular place, you will want to have a regular time to pray. Even if you have just five minutes a day for formal prayer, reserve it. Keep it sacred. Don't let anyone steal it from you.

I pray early in the morning. My body is conditioned to wake at 6:00 A.M., no matter what time zone I'm in. I get my coffee and my Bible, and I'm ready to meet God. Your schedule and physical makeup may be different from mine. If you're alert late at night, meet God then. Others use their coffee break time and meet God at their desk. Pray when it works best for you.

Many have to pray when driving to work. The radio is off and the windows shut out the traffic noise. You can make the steering wheel a prayer altar. I find even when I've prayed in my quiet time at home, I like to pray in my Suburban. Or you can pray during your evening walk, as you go by your neighbor's homes and thank God for the lovely flowers He made. Develop the art of praying everywhere, at all times, about everything.

Let me say a word about posture. When I was young, I knelt all the time. Now that I'm older, the knees rebel. I still kneel sometimes, but I sit a lot more than I used to. But that's all right; remember, "David went in and sat before the Lord" (2 Sa 7:18). Your posture is not the key. Any posture in prayer is acceptable if it's before the Lord. You can kneel, stand, sit, walk, or lie prostrate on the ground. I've done them all. Let your outward posture reflect your inner attitude of spirit.

Prayer is at the foundation of your Christian health. When you pray, you grow. When you stop praying, your faith shrivels up. The poet is absolutely right who wrote, "More things are wrought by prayer than this world dreams of."[1] One of my favorite statements is "Nothing of eternal consequence happens apart from prayer."

Developing an Effective Prayer Life

To develop a more effective prayer life, follow this simple outline. First, *obey Jesus and bring your requests to Him*. Jesus told us, "Whatever you ask in My name, that I will do" (Jo 14:13). If we don't ask, we aren't obedient. Then remember what James said in his epistle, "You do not have because you do not ask" (Jam 4:2).

Some have asked, and yet they did not get what they requested. Perhaps they didn't think God could do what they asked, or they thought God would not do it. Perhaps their problem is unbelief. If your request is centered in the will of God, then you must believe you will get it before God will give it to you. Jesus said, "Whatever things you ask when you pray, believe that you receive them, and you will have them" (Mk 11:24).

In the late 1970s we were praying for five million dollars to complete seven dormitories at Liberty University®. I knew God would give it to us. I remember praying, "Lord, give us the money so we can train over 1,200 young people to influence the world." I knew that's what God wanted to do, so I prayed confidently.

A skeptical reporter asked my wife, Macel, if I really believed the $5 million would come in. She said, "Jerry really believes it'll come in." The reporter continued to pry, "Is there a little crack in his confidence?" Again Macel answered, "Jerry knows God will send in $5 million because that money is needed to house an additional 1,200 students who can be trained for ministry." She explained that since training young people for ministry was God's will, the money would come in.

A colleague said he just didn't have faith for that much money, so I told him to pray for faith instead of money. Then I heard him pray what the disciples requested of Jesus, "Increase our faith" (Lk 17:5). Next, he confessed his weakness, "Lord, I believe; help my unbelief!" (Mk 9:24). Ask for more faith so you can pray for bigger things.

Some people don't get what they request because they ask for selfish reasons, or for worldly pleasures. The Bible describes this, "You ask and do not receive, because you ask amiss, that you may spend it on your pleasures" (Jam 4:3).

The second step is to *ask for things that God has promised to give.* Jesus said, "If . . . My words abide in you, you will ask what you desire, and it shall be done for you" (Jo 15:7). This means when the Bible influences your thinking—it abides in you—the Bible will guide you to pray for right things. I've found that the closer my request gets to the Bible, the more likely God will listen to my request. Then I'm able to get what I ask from God.

I shouldn't have to mention this, but sin in your life will block answers to your prayers. The Bible says, "We know that God does not hear sinners" (Jo 9:31). So, deal with your sin before you ask God for anything. The Bible says, "If I regard iniquity in my heart, the Lord will not hear [me]" (Ps 66:18). Don't let your sin keep you from answered prayer.

Thomas Road Baptist Church and Liberty University® are a direct result of God's answers to people's prayers. Nothing would have been accomplished without the prayers of my mother and the prayers of hundreds and thousands of others. For the Christian, prayer is vital. Paul wrote to the first century church in Thessalonica, "Pray without ceasing" (1 Th 5:17). And Jesus Himself promised us "Whatever things you ask in prayer, believing, you will receive" (Ma 21:22).

At the heart of reaching your *life purpose* is faithful, believing prayer. If you want to accomplish everything God has put in your heart, then give attention to your prayer life. Jesus said, "You must always pray" (Lk 18:1, *My Translation*).

Experiencing Faith

Begin keeping a prayer record. Some call this a journal, which is another word for a diary. Others record their answers next to their written prayer requests. That becomes their journal.

Begin writing your long prayer list of the names of family and friends. You won't make a complete list in one day. As you pray daily, other names will come to mind, so leave space to add additional names. If there's been any great answer to prayer in the past with any of these, make a notation of what happened next to each name.

On a separate page, *begin writing your short prayer list of current problems and projects.* As God begins to answer, make a notation of what happened. Some answers to prayer come in separate stages. You could have as many as three or four notations to one prayer request.

Begin journaling on a separate page. My wife tells me that women are more likely to do this than men because women are more reflective. But I do it, so we can all do it and we can all benefit. Your journal may include some background to wonderful answers to prayer. It may also include your insight into Bible study, as well as the lessons God is teaching you through prayer and witnessing.

Journaling can help you with major decision-making. Write down the strengths of both sides on a decision, then pray over them; asking God to help you make the right decision. I find that writing both sides of an issue helps me see the issue more objectively, and that helps me make the correct decision.

In my lifetime I've read from some of the published journals of great heroes of faith. I've learned some important lessons looking over their shoulders as they pour out their souls on paper. However, you're not writing a journal for anyone to read, so don't worry about grammar or word selection, just write what God is saying to you. Your journal will be private.

Two things will happen when you journal. First, you'll clarify your thoughts because, "Thoughts disentangle themselves when they pass through the lips and the fingertips."[2] Then you can build on your insight to reach higher in understanding. Second, your written thoughts will encourage you to greater faith when you come back later to read what God has done.

If you're interested in researching other journals, visit any of the following examples:

George Washington's Prayer Journal:
    (http://personal.pitnet.net/primarysources/george.html).
Missionary outreach:
    (www.abwe.org/pray/journal.asp)
The diary of David Brainerd:
    http://www.sermonindex.net/modules/newbb/
    viewtopic.php?topic_id=1866&forum=35&0
The Journal of George Fox, founder of the Quaker Movement:
    http://www.strecorsoc.org/gfox/gf_index.html

Suggested Reading: Luke 11:1–13

DAY 11

Growing Through Steps of Faith

> "Since you excel in so many ways, grow in faith."
>
> (2 Co 8:7, *My Translation*)

As a Christian, you will want to grow and stretch to learn new lessons and do new tasks. Today's lesson suggests ways to grow your faith and begin walking in some new, uncharted areas. I want to use my first experience of preaching on radio and TV in 1956 to challenge you to learn new lessons, just as I had to learn new lessons.

God continually pushes us out of our comfort zones and into a new challenge. And when a challenge is bigger than our ability to handle it, we'll grow our faith as we attempt to do this new task.

Preaching on radio and TV as a young pastor was the biggest challenge of my life—at least up until then. Now I look back and see how small was my step of faith. But that's the beauty of a loving God who teaches us to take small steps of faith so that later we can take bigger steps. When we see a small baby taking its first steps, we think, *That's no big deal for us.* But to the baby, first steps are the biggest victory in life.

What's your next challenge? We've been talking about writing down your *life purpose* and then writing your *life plan.* Today, let's talk about some of the first steps toward your goal in life. As you read my story, look for things that'll prepare you to handle bigger challenges.

A Giant Step of Faith

I had visited thousands of homes door-to-door in Lynchburg, inviting people—person-to-person—to attend my church. As a new pastor, my goal was to knock on the doors of one hundred homes every day of the week. In every home I visited the radio was blaring, and almost everyone had a radio in their car. At first it didn't cross my mind to use radio in my own local ministry, even though God had used the radio broadcasts of Charles Fuller and the "Old Fashioned Revival Hour" to prepare me for salvation.

Then one afternoon in the fall of 1956, Macel and I were listening to music on WBRG 1050 on the AM dial. It was a new country and western station that went on the air shortly after we began Thomas Road Baptist Church. I decided to begin my own daily broadcast on that station. Our church was small, just over one hundred people, and I didn't have any idea how to get started. I had no radio experience. I had never even visited a radio station.

I put on my best suit and tie, gathered a handful of Thomas Road Baptist Church weekly newsletters, and drove to the station to see the owner about buying time.

I was thinking we could afford a weekly program on Sunday mornings. But Mr. Epperson, owner of the station, a devout Christian layman, had a better idea. "Go on radio every day, Reverend," he advised me. "I've been looking for someone to start our broadcast day with words to the wise. You would be just perfect."

I swallowed hard, screwed up my courage, and asked him how much a daily program would cost. I had no idea how much radio time cost.

"How about seven dollars a program?" he answered. "Could your new church handle that?"

We shook hands and began a relationship that lasted many years. I began each broadcast day with a thirty-minute program live from the studio. WBRG had only 1,000 watts, but on a clear morning those watts carried our broadcast from the studio in Madison Heights, Virginia, to homes throughout Lynchburg and across Amherst and Campbell County. It reached thirty or forty miles to the foothills of the Blue Ridge Mountains.

The studio was in a little four-room prefab house on a large empty unpaved lot in the shadow of the transmitter, which was nothing but a tall, rather spindly broadcast tower. I sat at a metal desk in a studio no bigger than a large closet. My engineer sat across from me behind a glass window. In the summer when the sun rose early, our broadcast began at 6:30 A.M. As the fall and winter approached and the days grew shorter, my broadcast began at seven.

To get started, I signaled the engineer to play my theme song. These forty-nine years later I can't even remember what it was. But I still remember the excitement I felt when the record began to spin and the choir began to sing. After the theme song, I reported what God was doing in our church. I told about the excitement of the services and told stories about people whose lives were being changed by God through our congregation's ministry.

Next, I signaled the engineer to play the special song of that broadcast day. At first, I used records featuring the music of George Beverly Shea, who sang for Billy Graham, and other popular gospel singers of that day. In later broadcasts I used prerecorded soloists or groups of singers from Thomas Road Baptist Church. The last twenty minutes I preached and promoted the church. Then I rushed from the studio at the close of the broadcast to begin my 100 door-to-door visits for that day. I often told listeners which area of town I would be visiting, and when I arrived people would be waiting to greet me or ask me about our church.

Radio did something for the church immediately that I had not expected. All I had wanted to do by radio was to get people saved and invite them to the church. But the radio took me beyond the limits of my city. I was no longer focusing only on "Jerusalem and Judea" that was mentioned in Acts 1:8. I began getting letters, phone calls, and church visitors from outside Greater Lynchburg. Some came from almost fifty miles away. People came to my church from little towns I hadn't even thought about visiting.

I don't think it was my preaching that brought them. I was just an average preacher in those early days. They came because of the excitement of what God was doing at Thomas Road Baptist Church. When I told of drunks being saved and drying out, I also told of others struggling with problems who visited our services looking for help. And I told how God was putting families back together. Those looking for help began attending Thomas Road Baptist Church. Those were exciting days. Every time we had a conversion—breakthrough—I'd get on the radio to tell the area what God was doing.

Radio expanded my horizons and allowed me to perfect my broadcast skills. Yet I feel it's not the communication skills that God uses. Success comes when you share what God says in His Word and when you give testimony of what God is doing in the lives of His people.

Forty-nine dollars a week was a lot of money in those days. I gulped when I realized it meant two hundred dollars a month. We weren't spending that much money on anything—including building payments. But Mr. Epperson helped me take the step of faith by breaking a large payment into small bite-size pieces— seven dollars a day. Giant leaps of faith are sometimes taken in small daily steps. By faith I made the leap, knowing God would provide for our needs. In those early days, I learned the truth of Philippians 4:19, "And my God shall supply all your need according to His riches in glory by Christ Jesus."

Trusting God for Bigger Things

New steps of faith are not about the things you do, but they're about God working in you. Your main emphasis is never on the things you do or the preparation you make. Although these things are important, "it is God who works in you both to will and to do for His good pleasure" (Ph 2:13).

God put in me a desire to reach more people, and I took a step of faith to do His will. When God puts a desire in you to do a task for Him, two things will happen. First, God will help you do it. Second, you'll grow your faith to trust Him for bigger things in the future.

Most of the local barbershops turned on my radio program when customers talked about what was happening at our church. I never intended to "steal sheep," but the radio made them curious. Then they visited our church because we were doing more than any other church in town. These barbershops did another thing for our church. I'd call the names over the radio of those who got saved. Lynchburg is a small town, and inevitably, those in the barbershops knew the new converts or knew about them. And the same thing happened in the ladies' beauty shops. I was spreading revival excitement and didn't even know it.

Immediately people began attending because of the radio program. Offerings went up. I took a leap of faith, but within a few months I realized radio was my way to reach my Jerusalem, my Judea, and the state of Virginia.

As you look at your *life purpose*, focus on God and His plan for your life. Every step of faith you take is about Him and what He wants to do in your life. Don't worry about God's provision. God will provide if you've focused on Him. In what areas are you holding back in fear that this dream is really too big, or in uncertainty whether God will provide?

Experiencing Faith

Review. Look over your one-sentence statement of your *life purpose*. Make sure this is what God wants for your life. Next, review your *life plan*. Make sure you know the direction God wants you to go.

Look for your challenges. Make a list of two or three steps of faith that are facing you both now and in the distant future. As you write these down, what you must do will become clearer in your mind.

Focus on one step of faith. Just as a baby learning to walk can't take three steps at one time, so you shouldn't try to focus on all your challenges at one time. Pray over the list and target one challenge for today. Here's what you can do about that challenge:

Pray—ask God to help you know what to do.

Aim—focus on what you want to accomplish with this step of faith.

Determine—decide what is the first thing to do.

Count the cost—figure out the problems or consequences from taking this step.

Pray again—ask God to help you and to guide each step you take.

You never determine to grow your faith for its own sake, although you want to become a greater man or woman of faith. You focus on God and take a step that you think He wants you to take. And just as any walking or running steps will make your body stronger, so each step will make your faith stronger. And when you go from one faith project to another, you grow "from faith to faith" (Ro 1:17).

Suggested Reading: Acts 16:6–40

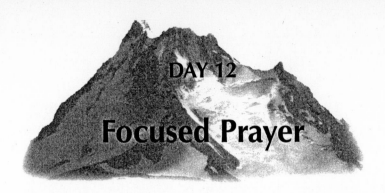

DAY 12

Focused Prayer

> "Therefore do not be unwise, but understand what the will of the Lord is."
>
> (Ep 5:17)

S ometimes you must focus all your prayer energy on one thing, an emergency. This could be a financial crisis, a health crisis, or a problem where you work. You do not just pray about the issue once during your quiet time. No, you become desperate about the crisis.

Remember when Peter got out of the boat to walk on the water to Jesus (Ma 14:29). He was doing something that had never been done before. Peter defied gravity. The secret of walking on water was going to Jesus. He began to sink when he took his eyes off Jesus, "when he saw that the wind was boisterous" (v. 30). Notice his desperate prayer, "Lord, save me" (v. 30).

Your crisis may be an instant emergency when you don't have time to confess sins to get on "praying ground," nor do you have the opportunity to properly approach God. Just cry out, "Help!"

Your crisis may be way off in the future, but you know it's coming. Your crisis may be a decision that will determine your future life, such as marriage or accepting a job in a distant city. One crisis I faced was determining my life's work. I was approaching college graduation without knowing what I'd do, or where I'd do it.

The First Big Challenge

As I came to the end of my Bible college training, I didn't know what I was going to do. I had never preached a Sunday morning sermon to a congregation. My speech and preaching classes at Baptist Bible College gave me the opportunity to preach to professors and to my peers, but that was no proof that I could preach a real sermon to real people sitting in real pews and make a difference in their lives. I was afraid to make a decision about any future ministry until I knew for certain whether God could use my preaching ability.

During my senior year at Baptist Bible College, I was the weekend youth pastor at Kansas City Baptist Temple. Each week I drove 180 miles from Springfield, Missouri, to Kansas City to minister to the youth of that church. Then without warning, just two weeks before my graduation, Pastor Zimmerman told me that I would be taking his place in the pulpit that next Sunday morning. He didn't ask me if I wanted to preach or if I could preach or if it would be convenient for me to preach that Sunday. He simply told me I would be preaching next week, and that was that. I drove back to college in shock and surprise.

The Kansas City church was large and intimidating. There were well over a thousand in attendance. It was one of the great churches of America where the great pulpiteers often preached. What could I do in the face of such a great tradition?

At a time of crisis, the first thing a Christian does is to pray. I had prayed the sinner's prayer at the altar of Park Avenue Baptist Church and developed the habit of conversational prayer in the months that followed. I had learned to intercede regularly for my Sunday school class, but it was during this eventful week in 1956 that I really began to pray in earnest.

I prayed non-stop that week, asking God to use the experience to show me His will for my life. I prayed about a text from which I would preach. As I studied the related Scriptures, I prayed about each one of them. As I wrote my outline, I prayed about each point. And as I filled in the illustrations, I drenched each one in prayer.

This would be my first real sermon. I was frightened and unsure that I could do it. The people of Baptist Temple in Kansas City had heard the greatest preachers. How could I follow them? My knees knocked and my palms grew damp at the very thought of preaching before that many people.

In some churches there is no way to really measure a sermon's effectiveness. Preachers preach, and after the benediction the congregation goes home. But in the Baptist Temple in Kansas City—whether right or wrong—there was a standard by which every sermon was judged. That test of a sermon's effectiveness continues in most Baptist churches to this day.

After each sermon an invitation was given for people to come to the front of the auditorium. There, people responded to accept Christ as Savior, to seek a deeper spiritual life, to be baptized, or to register for membership. Even though there were hundreds of people in attendance that Sunday morning, if no one came forward my first sermon would be considered a flop. So I prayed and I worried. I didn't just want people to come forward to join the church or get baptized; I wanted someone to find Christ as Savior through my preaching. If no one came forward to be born again, I would consider the sermon a failure.

I begged God to show me through this single sermon if He was calling me to preach and to pastor a church. "Show me clearly, Lord . . . so clearly that I cannot misunderstand what You are saying."

I fasted and prayed the last three days before my sermon. On Saturday night I prayed almost all night long, from sunset until sunrise. Gradually my fear lifted. On Sunday morning when I stood to speak before that large crowd of people, I felt perfectly calm. I announced my text from Hebrews and preached with a sense of total freedom. My throat wasn't dry. My palms weren't sweaty. I felt alive and at home in the pulpit; and the people, even the young ones, listened attentively.

When the invitation was given, nineteen people responded to

give their lives to Christ, an average response for a Sunday morning service at Baptist Temple. As I stood at the altar shaking hands with the seekers and introducing them to the deacons who would counsel them, I continued to pray that God's will would be perfectly clear.

The last person in line was a wrinkled old lady I had seen a dozen or more times in the front rows of Baptist Temple. The dear old woman grasped my hand and leaned forward to whisper in my ear. "Young man," she said, her voice trembling slightly, "I am a charter member of this church. I've been sitting in these pews since Dr. Zimmerman started it. I've heard him preach and I've heard all the great preachers he's brought here, but this morning through your sermon God showed me for the first time that I've never really been born again." I felt her hands trembling in mine. She was blinking back her tears. I knew she was an authentic seeker, and when she asked, "Will you pray with me that I might be saved?" I knew that God had heard and answered my prayer for an unmistakable sign.

How to Focus Your Prayers

The key to developing healthy faith is knowing God will hear and answer when a crisis looms. The first thing is to *realize that prayer is about God and His purpose for your life.* Effective prayer is not primarily about getting what you want or what you need, although a problem may motivate you to deeper prayer. Remember, when you get on your knees before God it's about Him.

When you come to God, you are searching for His purpose, also called His will for your life. Since God tells us to know His will, you must believe God will show it to you. "Therefore do not be unwise, but understand what the will of the Lord is" (Ep 5:17). We begin by surrendering our will to His will. In the Lord's Prayer we ask, "Thy will be done" (Ma 6:10, KJV).

After you've yielded your present life to God's plan, then *start searching for God's will* in this matter by asking Him to show you what to do. David prayed, "Lead me, O Lord" (Ps 5:8), and to make sure he knew the path was God's will, he prayed, "Lead me in a plain path" (Ps 27:11, KJV).

Sometimes a prayer problem is so big that you must pray about it for a long time. Praying a long time means you pray repeatedly for God's direction. I like to paraphrase one of my favorite verses, "Pray continually in an intermittent way" (1 Th 5:17, *My Translation*). The King James reads, "Pray without ceasing." But you can't pray all the time, every day. Obviously, you've got a lot of family and business details that demand much of your attention. The original language suggests praying like a baby cries, not all the time; but when a baby needs something it cries. So this verse teaches one to pray every time you have a need. That's why I described this verse, "Pray intermittently."

So I spent a whole week praying about this sermon. Every time I prayed—before meals, between classes, and driving my car— I continually reminded God I wanted souls saved when I preached the following Sunday.

But there is a place for long prayers. I prayed almost all night before my first sermon. The Bible is filled with stories of people who spent a long time in prayer when faced with a problem. After Paul was converted on the road to Damascus, he spent three days in the presence of God (Ac 9:9). A believer named Ananias was sent by God to Paul and was told, "Behold he [Paul] is praying" (v. 11).

Spending a long time in prayer does something to you. It builds up your determination to see the issues brought to completion. Sometimes the more you pray, the stronger your faith becomes. When your faith is mature enough, "Whatever things you ask in prayer, believing, you will receive" (Ma 21:22).

Spending a long time in prayer demonstrates your sincerity to God. Paul at one place stated, "I am testing the sincerity of your love" (2 Co 8:8). Praying a long time shows God you are putting your whole life on the line to get an answer about this matter.

There is a final principle. ***Prayer should motivate you to action.***

The more I prayed for my sermon, the more I realized I had to study deeply. I studied more for that sermon than for anything else I had ever done for God. I found a double-edged sword cutting through my life. The more I prayed for the sermon, the more I realized I needed additional study to make it the best sermon I'd ever preached. And the more I studied, the more it drove me to continual prayer.

Experiencing Faith

Target one prayer burden. You have a whole list of things to pray for, but in this assignment ask God to show you one request that you must target. This assignment is not about your human desire, but something God wants you to have. Be sensitive to God's Spirit; choose a request that is important to God's kingdom. If it's only a "personal" request, you'll give up praying when the going gets rough. If God is leading you into focused prayer, then you'll get His supernatural help to pray through to victory.

Write the specific request on a separate page in your journal, separate from your usual prayer requests. Indicate why this is a special request, and also write down what answer you want God to give. When you pray exactly, you'll persevere in prayer.

Focus on time, place, and duration. We all have busy schedules, but find some time that you can give to God. If you have to, get up early in the morning to give time to God in prayer for that request. Make a note of the place where you will go to pray about this request, then note how much time you plan to spend on each occasion when you pray. Then determine how long you will be praying for this request: days, weeks, or months. Some requests have natural terminal dates, such as when I prayed all week for a specific Sunday result. I didn't pray past the target Sunday date.

Reflect. Think back to a past crisis or major prayer request. What did you do to get an answer from God? What has worked in the past can work again. Write down God's answer, because that way you won't forget it. Also, writing it down will motivate you to prayer, both this time and when the next crisis comes.

And there will be more problems in the future, because we don't live in a perfect world. "Man who is born of woman is of few days and full of trouble" (Job 14:1). Therefore, learn the lesson of focused prayer, because God will answer.

Suggested Reading: Matthew 14:22–33

DAY 13

Facing Obstacles

"When it was clear that he (Paul) wouldn't be dissuaded, we gave up and said, 'The will of the Lord be done.'"

(Ac 21:14, LB)

There's no such thing as a life without problems or obstacles. Gardens have weeds that need pulling, loved ones get sick, and every car will eventually break down and need repair. Ever since Adam and Eve fell in the Garden, we've had problems with sin and problems that come from living in a fallen world. Job tells us, "Man is born to trouble" (Job 5:7).

The Bible teaches that we have three opponents: the world, the flesh, and the devil (Ep 2:1–2; 4:27; 1 Jo 2:15–17). You must constantly be aware of the problems that sin introduces into your life, and you must overcome these problems by faith. As God solves your problems, your faith will grow stronger. If you're not on guard, many of these problems will weaken your faith.

If your faith was never tested, you wouldn't know if it was real. But "the testing of your faith produces patience . . . that you may be perfect and complete, lacking nothing" (Jam 1:3–4).

Today you may face a casual test of your faith, or it may be severe. When I began my church, I faced one of the most difficult tests of my life. I don't know what would have happened if I had let the opposition defeat me. So I've prepared this chapter to prepare you to face opposition to your faith.

Encountering Opposition

After I graduated from Baptist Bible College at age 22, I struggled for days whether to go start a church in Macon, Georgia, or help my friends start a church in Lynchburg. There was a "pull" in each direction, and the decision was difficult. After days of struggling I felt it was best to postpone any move to Georgia for at least a few months. As I prayed about it, I felt comfortable with the decision to help start a church in Lynchburg. Little did I know that decision would be severely tested with the biggest obstacle I'd faced since being a Christian.

I phoned the pastor of Park Avenue Baptist Church and asked to see him. That was an uncomfortable meeting because I represented members who had left the church because they disagreed with things that had developed in the church. We sat together in his little study just off the sanctuary where I had found Christ as Savior. The meeting was all the more uncomfortable because I loved Park Avenue Baptist Church.

"They're going to start a church anyway," I began. "And they've asked me to help them get it started. Why not turn this defeat into a victory? Let the second church be considered a mission church as a sister church of Park Avenue Baptist. We can pray and work together. Both churches will grow."

He listened silently while I reasoned on behalf of the new church. I tried to convince the pastor that if we worked together, we could turn this tragedy into another triumph for Christ and for His kingdom.

He listened and nodded silently. He knew that the thirty-five people were going to start their church. I reiterated their promises and assured him that we meant only good for the city, for the Kingdom, and for Park Avenue Baptist Church.

After an hour or so he seemed willing to give the plan a try. Then he excused himself, went to a nearby office, and called our fellowship's headquarters. I don't know whom he called that day or what exactly was said between them, but when he ended his call and came back into his office, he was no longer willing to cooperate.

An executive of our little Baptist fellowship (we didn't like to call ourselves a denomination and preferred to be seen as a "movement") passed on the word through him to me that our plan to begin another church in Lynchburg was "unacceptable" and that the only acceptable option I had was "to leave town immediately and to let them [the dissenters] go."

The pastor stood towering over me, voicing his authority and the authority of his mysterious contact at headquarters. He said if I stayed to help the church, I would be taking a stand against men I loved and respected in the Baptist Bible Fellowship.

Yet, if I let them scare me away, I would not be obedient to the voice of God. I had a growing confidence the Lord was calling me to stay in Lynchburg.

"I'm sorry," I told the pastor. "I mean you and your church no harm. But I will help the thirty-five people start a second church in Lynchburg. I cannot back away from that decision."

How lonely I felt that day, deciding against the advice of the new pastor of Park Avenue Baptist Church (Pastor Donnelson was no longer there) and the men who taught me at Baptist Bible College. After considering all the options, I knew that I wanted to stay in Lynchburg, at least for a while; and even as I prayed, I felt that God wanted me to stay as well.

The pastor saw my gesture as an attack against him and his congregation. He began to speak publicly against me and against the thirty-five dissenters. Word quickly spread to Springfield and throughout our little fellowship to key pastors and powerful Baptist leaders across the country.

One of the denomination's leaders called me from Springfield to warn me officially. "You stated that you planned to start a church in Macon, Georgia. You must keep your word."

I argued that I was needed in Lynchburg, at least temporarily. I explained that the people were going to start a second church whether I stayed or not, and that it seemed appropriate that someone who cared about both sides would help them in those crucial early weeks.

"Those people are troublemakers," he replied. "You should not help them start a church. And it won't help your future, either."

In spite of the menacing tones in the flurry of phone calls that followed, I stayed in Lynchburg. "If you do not leave Lynchburg immediately," one official caller informed me, "you will be cut off from the Baptist Bible Fellowship International. You will not be welcome to preach in our churches or to attend our fellowship meetings. We will not accept students at Baptist Bible College from your church, nor will our students be allowed to assist you in your ministry."

Those were terrible times for me. I had only been a Christian for four years. I had been converted through one of their churches and tutored by their ministers and lay leaders. I had been taught by their professors in their Bible college. I was grateful to them, and I was loyal to their school, to their missions program, and to their national leadership. But my heart and soul were wrapped up in that little congregation called Thomas Road Baptist Church. It was a real emotional blow to think that I would be cut off from all of that. (In the years since, this broken fellowship between the Baptist Bible Fellowship and this pastor has been totally healed.)

Staying on Track

Certain things happened to me in the next few weeks that helped me understand some important principles. I want to share these with you for the days when you face opposition about your decisions and the will of God. First, when dealing with opposition, *remember you belong to God alone and not to anything else on this earth.* People and organizations have to be secondary in your life. Opposition can remind you that you belong only to God. It is His voice in your heart and His Word that directs you.

Opposition is also a reminder to *look to the integrity of your heart.* When you feel cut off, isolated, and abandoned, the Psalms of David can express your need before God. "I cried out to God with my voice—to God with my voice; and He gave ear to me" (Ps 77:1). Examine the accusations and check your motives. Pray that God will give you the humility to listen and accept any truth in the criticism.

When opposition faces you, *recommit yourself to your life's priority.* I went to my childhood bedroom in the old family house, which was now my home in Lynchburg. I had lost every friend I had in the ministry. "God, I am Yours alone," I said. "Nobody else wants me. I am no longer the property of any church or any denomination or any movement. I am totally and entirely yours. I will minister to this city. You have called me here, and here I will stay. I will reach this town for Christ and I will do it all alone if that's what it takes."

When your faith is opposed, make sure your stand is grounded in the Bible. Look again at your *life purpose.* I've often said, "Make sure you're right, then go ahead." On June 24, 1956, those thirty-five adults held their first service in the Mountain View Elementary School auditorium. We rented the school for one Sunday. I preached. My future wife, Macel, played the piano. And our little congregation gathered and prayed together for God's guidance for our new church and for a home that we could call our own.

On the next rain-drenched day, Monday afternoon, I found myself with Percy Hall, who would become a deacon, driving about Lynchburg looking for a place to house our little congregation. Percy's insurance agent had told him that there was an empty building on Thomas Road in the undeveloped west end of Lynchburg. We parked in the rain and stared at the thirty-by-fifty-foot abandoned building standing on the corner of that muddy lot. In the early 1940s it had been a corner grocery store. In the early 1950s the building had housed the Donald Duck Bottling Company, a soft drink firm that went defunct.

We walked to the building, pushed open a back door, and brushed away the cobwebs and debris that stood directly in our pathway. The building was empty except for broken shelves, rusty pipes, and tattered boxes piled in one corner. A sticky coat of black syrup stained the floor and the walls and had even splashed up onto the ceiling. But we hardly noticed the mess. The possibilities of that filthy little building seemed endless, and the property surrounding it was entirely empty.

"Percy," I said excitedly, "let's find out who owns it; maybe this is the place to start."

The rent would be three hundred dollars a month. The thirty-six of us agreed to take on that expense among us. For the next week we shoveled and pounded and polished. We acquired old theater seats and set them in place. We hung curtains over broken or cracked windows. We collected hymnbooks and Bibles, and we moved an old upright piano to its place near the little wooden lectern that would serve as my first pulpit.

On Wednesday evening, June 27, our congregation met in the partially restored building to hold the organizational meeting of our new church. We adopted a simple constitution and bylaws. We elected our first three trustees and named ourselves the Thomas Road Baptist Church. Again we prayed that God would lead us from the very first moment of our ministry in Lynchburg. We didn't do anything without praying about it first. We believed that God was there with us from the beginning, and we asked Him to guide us each step of the way.

On July 1, 1956, our first Sunday service was held on Thomas Road in Lynchburg. At 6:30 A.M. that first Sunday morning, I awakened in our home on Rustburg Road to the smell of biscuits, gravy, and bacon. By 8:15 A.M. I was unlocking the old building. I pulled back the curtains so that the sun would stream into our rough little sanctuary and take off the morning chill. I arranged and rearranged the seats. I placed my Bible on the little pulpit and opened it to my morning text. I paced up and down the center aisle, nervously praying, occasionally looking down Thomas Road for any sign that someone would actually show up that day.

When we finally began our Sunday school that first Sunday morning, there were thirty-five adults and three dozen or more children in attendance. I greeted each one as he or she entered. I explained how we would divide the room into sections for our first class meetings. We took a Sunday school offering and sang happy birthday to a child. There was a short break after Sunday school.

Then came the first church service in our own building. I remember praying the pastoral prayer, reading my text, Philippians 3:12–14, and beginning to preach my first sermon on Thomas Road. That storefront church looked very much like a cathedral to me. And the sun shone through the cracked windows, making streaks of light in the dust that still shimmered in the air. The people sat in pools of light beaming up at me. It was our first Sunday, and everybody was on his or her best behavior. No baby cried that morning. No child squirmed. No adult dozed off.

I did the right thing by staying in Lynchburg. God has spread the gospel throughout the world from Thomas Road Baptist Church. This last principle has guided my life ever since: *Make a decision, then make it work.* We've surely done that.

Experiencing Faith

Objectify. Perhaps the thing that scares you most about opposition is that you don't really understand what's going on around you. We're usually more afraid of things we can't see than we are of things we know about. Sometimes we're really afraid when we fully know, but most of the time our fears are exaggerated or unfounded.

Write in your journal the exact nature of an opposition that you presently face. Answer these questions in your journal: Why am I being opposed? Who is behind the opposition? What will happen if I give in to the opposition? What will happen if I don't give in to the opposition?

Develop a prayer strategy. When you have objectified your opposition, you now can pray intelligently about the problem. Instead of praying, "God help me," you should pray for the exact results you want God to give you. Jesus said, "Ask, and it will be given to you" (Ma 7:7).

Determine what you'll do and how you'll react. Don't wait until you are in the fire to determine how you'll react. Write in your journal what will be your reaction.

Make your challenge a matter of faith. After you've written your reaction in your journal, pray for God to give you the strength to react in a Christian way. "I can do all things through Christ who strengthens me" (Ph 4:13).

Rejoice in opposition. None of us likes to rejoice in hard times, but that's what Peter tells us to do. "Do not think it strange concerning the fiery trial which is to try you, as though some strange thing happened to you; but rejoice to the extent that you partake of Christ's sufferings" (1 Pe 4:12–13). When you can rejoice in adversity, your faith will grow (Jam 1:2–5).

Suggested Reading: Acts 11:19–30

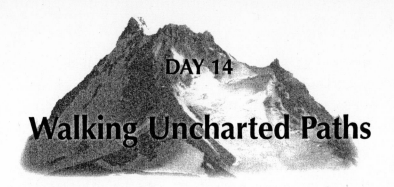

DAY 14

Walking Uncharted Paths

"By faith Abraham obeyed when he was called to go out to the place which he would receive as an inheritance. And he went out, not knowing where he was going."

(He 11:8)

Sometimes it seems as though life is going smoothly, predictably, with no major obstacles. But gradually or suddenly, it's time for a life change. Perhaps the change is just a major addition to the current life you're living—the birth of twins, a doubled client base. Other times the dream takes you in a whole new direction—a marriage proposal, a cross-country move, a child with a major disability. The change may look good or bad, but it's clearly God's will for you.

A New Dream

When I began broadcasting daily on radio, it never once crossed my mind to preach on television. No one was preaching the gospel on television; there wasn't even an occasional gospel broadcast like a Billy Graham Crusade. When I first began making my evangelistic visits in the homes, I noticed the radio was the central focus of the home. Even though it was playing when I visited a home, it didn't interfere with my conversation.

But shortly after I began, television became the focus of the family. Television was different; people wouldn't turn off the TV to talk with me, and its presence was a distraction. Television became an obstacle, and some wanted to stay home on Sunday evenings to watch TV. Instead of getting angry with television or irritated with a family, I began asking how I could turn this obstacle into a tool for the Kingdom.

I'm sure I said a few times, "It would be wonderful if a preacher could preach the gospel over television." As that idle statement became a dream, I thought, *Why not me?*

At first I thought television time would cost too much, and then I reminded myself, "God can do anything." I believed He could put our little church on television, even though no one to my knowledge had ever done it. I prayed, Macel prayed, and the group of men who started the church with me prayed.

In October 1956 I decided it was time to act on my dream. One Monday morning I drove to the small studio and office building of our ABC television affiliate, WLVA. In those days Channel 13 was as primitive for a television station as our storefront building was for a church.

The studio was in a small makeshift downtown building on Church Street. Often there was only one working black-and-white camera and a one- or two-man crew. One person would set the lights and microphones and run between the two cameras (if both were working). The other employee ran the control panel.

The station offered to sell me a half-hour time slot each week for ninety dollars, almost twice what the church was paying for radio time. I signed the contract immediately and agreed to report to the studio that next Sunday afternoon for a 5:30 P.M. live telecast.

We had no soloists at the church at that time, so I asked a young man, Bill Brooks, who was at the Methodist church to sing. Macel agreed to accompany him on the out-of-tune upright piano in the tiny studio. Together the three of us launched our television ministry, in those days simply called "Thomas Road Baptist Church Presents."

Late on Sunday afternoon Macel, Bill, and I arrived at the studio with absolutely no instructions as to what we were going to do. At

5:30 P.M. a red light came on at the studio door, and the camera-man/director pointed at me to begin the program. "Hello," I said, swallowing hard and looking to Macel and Bill for support. "My name is Jerry Falwell. I am the pastor of the Thomas Road Baptist Church."

I began the program, telling about our congregation and its services. I told how many new visitors were crowding into our little sanctuary and how many people were praying to receive Christ. I told about the growth of our Sunday school and of the small tent we had erected for our expanding children's department. I excitedly told how we had already begun construction on a new auditorium that would double our seating capacity.

After the solo, I opened my Bible and delivered a short sermon. As we signed off, Macel played and I took one last opportunity to invite those viewing to visit Thomas Road Baptist Church that very evening. "Tonight," I said, "in just ninety minutes, I will be preaching from the Bible story of Jeremiah at our church on Thomas Road. You have plenty of time to eat a peanut butter sandwich, drink a glass of milk, grab your Bible, and come on over! I'll welcome you personally, so please stop me at the door to tell me you heard me on television."

And the people came in crowds. No other preachers were on television then. Television made me a kind of an instant celebrity to the unsaved. To Christians, I was carrying their banner to reach the lost. After radio, this was the second greatest method that God used to build our church.

When God originally created all things, He created radio waves and television waves. God created DNA, the atom that produces nuclear energy, and the possibility of the computer chip. New technology doesn't catch God by surprise. But quickly I found some Christians fighting TV because Satan was "the god of the air (waves)." The issue was not really television technology, but the producers of harmful programs, sexually explicit scenes, violence, anti-godly heroes, cursing, etc. So, let's not just curse the darkness, but light a candle; let's use technology for the glory of God.

With a microphone, I can preach to more people on one Sunday than the apostle Paul preached to in his lifetime. With a television camera I can go into homes, bars, political offices—anywhere. I can preach the gospel across state lines, national boundaries, and ethnic barriers. Today the Old-Time Gospel Hour television program can be seen weekly in every American home and on every continent except Antarctica.

A New Step of Faith

What new challenge are you facing? In what ways is God leading you to new adventures and new tests of faith? With this lesson, I want to stretch your faith to believe God to walk an uncharted path. I have some principles to help you think creatively about stepping out into the unknown. First, *remember that everything God does revolves around people.* Shortly after I began my church, other pastors were complaining that their people were staying home on Sunday evenings to watch television. My strategy was not a new church program or new religious technique. My focus was on people. I intended to go where the people were and to minister to them on their own turf.

If you're a part of a church that's struggling, remember the solution is people. Not programs. If you love people, help people, and speak to the heart of people, there'll be love and vitality in what you do. If you face a medical or financial crisis, keep your eye on what God wants to do through you and those around you, not on the technical, grim details.

When you think about going into uncharted waters, look back to your *life purpose.* Will this new step of faith help accomplish it? If it does, move ahead.

Next, ask where God's plan is in this. When you look at uncharted waters, the first questions are not, How much money will it cost? Who will help me? Or, What is the location, or the equipment I will need? When you look at your limitations, you're not looking by faith. Your first question should be, "Is

God in it?" Faith is doing what God tells you. Obviously, money, location, help, and equipment are all factors. But they're not the deciding factors. If God is in it . . . if people will be helped . . . if it fits scriptural boundaries . . . if you've prayed . . . then move ahead!

The second principle is to *think big.* I needed to think beyond the little Donald Duck building on Thomas Road. As soon as television syndication became available, I began expanding our television program to other cities in Virginia: Roanoke, Charlottesville, Richmond, and beyond. When the satellite dish became available, I preached the gospel live to every time zone in the United States. Finally, the world.

Finally, *minister with no thought of limitation or letup.* I once told a group of pastors the keys to building a church were (1) contacting people, (2) continuously contacting people, (3) with no consciousness of limiting or stopping. I would give the same advice to you, whether you are in business or going into other ventures. If you know you're right, then go ahead.

Experiencing Faith

Start right. Before launching out into uncharted areas, you need to know your launching pad. That's another way of saying you must know who you are, what your *life purpose* is, and why you are launching into something. Will this activity please God? And does this path lead you toward your *life purpose* or dream? If you don't get good answers to these questions, you need to stop and pray more about the plan. Perhaps you should put off your launch date.

Write your *life purpose* in your journal again, then write how this step into uncharted paths fulfills your dream. If you can't tie the two together, slow down.

The next action point is to *list the results you expect from stepping out by faith* into this uncharted path. Then look at the results and ask if the "reward-risk" ratio is worth it. Are the rewards you will gain worth the risk of things you will lose? Hard question, but a necessary one at this juncture.

Some risks are not worth the effort, or may not be appropriate at this time. Waiting can be a good test to be sure God is in the venture. Sometimes a future day will give you clearer insight than you have today. So wait, but don't just twiddle your thumbs. Pray and seek God's leadership while waiting for full confidence.

Wait until you know it's God's will, and then launch out. Some people are afraid to take risks. They're afraid of losing money, or reputation, or something else valuable to them. It's an inner thing; they are just not risk-takers. Their answer is not to look within and "pump up their courage," but rather, to look without. When we look to God before launching into uncharted waters, it's an act of faith. When we know what God wants us to do, then we can step out in His confidence and obey Him. If we step out in our confidence, we might fail. So make sure God has spoken, then go ahead.

Suggested Reading: Acts 5:17–42

DAY 15

How Can I Have More Faith?

"As newborn babes, desire the pure milk of the word, that you may grow thereby."

(1 Pe 2:2)

Through the years, I have had presidents, senators, and business moguls ask me, "How can I have more faith?" I always answer them by pointing to the Bible and saying, "To get more faith, you've got to get more of this." Then I quote what Paul said, "Faith [comes] by hearing, and hearing by the word of God" (Ro 10:17).

I explain to everyone that "faith is doing what God wants us to do." I go on to explain that the more we learn about God in the Bible, the better we can trust Him. Also, when the Bible influences us—influences our thinking and attitudes—we can pray according to God's will and get our prayers answered.

Two weeks ago you started this faith journey. You've been reading about determining your life purpose and developing giant faith. You've been seeing many ways God teaches us about faith. You've even read some stories telling how I took a few leaps into the darkness and took some giant leaps of faith.

In this chapter I want to give you some simple steps to developing your faith further. You don't have to lead a large, growing church and university to get door-opening faith. You could be a widow on a fixed income, yet you could develop the strongest faith of anyone on earth. How? When the teachings of the Bible completely control your entire life, you do exactly what God wants you to do all the time. And that's my definition of faith: "Faith is doing what God wants you to do."

Let's go back to the beginning of my Christian experience to see how God taught me the Bible.

Learning the Bible Increases Faith

When I first got saved, the Bible seemed too large, too long, too difficult to ever read from cover to cover, let alone to understand. But I saw all the members of Park Avenue Baptist Church bringing a Bible to church, and I went to my youth pastor, Jack Dinsbeer, to ask about the Bible.

He told me, "You will want to read the whole Bible, but don't try to read the whole Bible at one time. You wouldn't read one of your textbooks at school in one sitting, would you?"

During the first few days of my Christian life, I read through the Gospels. Shortly thereafter, I heard someone say I should also read five psalms and one chapter of Proverbs every day. I immediately began on that program.

I circled key verses in my Bible and memorized them. Next, I began to sample the Old Testament stories of the great heroes of faith. They stretched my imagination.

Then one day, Jack Dinsbeer helped me design a lifelong program for reading and studying the Bible, and I have maintained that program for these fifty-three years. By reading just three chapters a day and five chapters on Sunday, I read the Bible completely through every year. But almost every day of the year I read more than that, never less. I also read (almost every day) five chapters in the Psalms and one chapter from Proverbs. This way, I read through both books every month.

The Psalms motivate me to worship and praise. When the enemy is close on my trail, there is nothing like the Psalms to help me feel the presence of God. That perks me up and renews my courage and determination. The Proverbs are rich in practical wisdom and full of humor.

I look back on long Bible discussions with my youth pastor as a foundation for my spiritual life. Jack didn't just lecture me about the Bible; he let me ask questions. He told me where the answers were in the Bible. Together we looked them up in our Bibles. It was my first opportunity to see someone use a concordance (a book that lists every word in the Bible with its reference: book, chapter, and verse). If Dinsbeer couldn't remember an entire verse, one word would send him thumbing through his concordance in search of the text we needed.

Very early I became a teacher. As soon as I learned one simple truth from the Bible, Jack would have me teach it to the others at a youth meeting or as a substitute teacher for a Sunday school class. "You learned it," he would say. "Now share it with somebody else." I quickly found that teaching the Bible was an outstanding way to master its contents.

I like to read the Bible with my needs in focus. I continually ask, "How can I apply this to my life?" and "What does God want me to do with this truth?" This means I am reading for my own spiritual growth.

Some people get up every day, open the Bible, and let a finger drop onto the passage they will read and study for that day. Although this doesn't have much system and discipline, it's better than not reading at all. Others begin with a book in the Bible and read until they complete it or lose interest. Then they begin again somewhere else. I would suggest you have a planned reading program that you faithfully maintain.

I start in Genesis and Matthew simultaneously and read the Old and New Testaments in sequential order from the beginning to the end. I jot down the dates of each reading and many of the inspiring ideas God gives me along the way. I keep a legal pad nearby for writing longer notes, ideas for lessons, sermons, a book, or an article. You will want to keep any such notes in your journal.

I soon learned to combine my prayer time and my Bible reading. I talk to God as I read the Bible. Early in my Christian life I spent ten or fifteen minutes with God. Within a short time, I was spending thirty minutes each morning in prayer and Bible reading.

For fifty-three years I have continued that habit. Almost every day there is a good reason not to do it. There is an assignment due, a crisis waiting, a family matter that needs attention, a breakfast meeting, or a conference call. The demands of each new day would destroy my time alone with God and His Word if I let them. But I dare not. When I fail to keep my appointed time, it cripples the day.

If you let several days pass without Bible reading and prayer, the damage will accumulate, and your spiritual life will bog down noticeably.

Four Truths About Faith

I remember the first time I was asked about developing stronger faith. It was so challenging that I never forgot the incident. Years ago I was visiting a distraught mother in the emergency room of the hospital. After I prayed for her daughter to recover from a terrible accident, she asked, "How can I have deeper faith?" I wanted to answer her but didn't know how. I had never thought about the question. She added, "If I had more faith, I could pray her through this crisis."

Since I always talk to God about these things, I immediately asked God—silently—to give me an answer for the mother. Then God brought a Bible verse to my mind. I told the mother the same thing I later told national leaders. "You can get more faith from the Word of God." I held up the Bible I was carrying and said, "You get faith from this."

Then I quoted for her the verse I quoted earlier: "Faith comes by hearing, and hearing by the word of God" (Ro 10:17). I explained that when we obey His instructions in the Bible, we are acting in faith. I told her she needed to read and study the Bible to know the way God does things. Then I said, "The better you understand the Bible, the better you understand God; then you can pray for healing and deliverance for your daughter."

After this incident, I realized that four basic truths will help you grow a greater and stronger faith as you do your reading and Bible study. First, remember that the Bible is called "the word of faith" (Ro 10:8; 1 Ti 4:6). This means *the Bible contains information about the Christian faith.* When we're pouring the Bible into our minds, we're pouring faith into our hearts. The Bible tells us who God is and how He does things. When we know the Bible well, we know how God does things. We are living by faith when we fit into God's way of doing things.

But the Bible is more than stories and information about God. The second truth is to know that *God has imbedded His presence in the words of God.* This is called the inspiration of Scripture: "All Scripture is given by inspiration of God" (2 Ti 3:16). The word *inspiration* is more than the enthusiasm of the author coming through when you read his message. Inspiration means "to breathe." When God inspired the words of Scripture, He breathed His presence into the words. When I read the Bible and believe it, I am receiving God into my life. When I have God, I have the true source of faith. The more I get of God from the Bible, the more my faith grows.

The third point is to understand that *the Bible has life—God's life— in its words.* Jesus said of His words, "The words that I speak to you are spirit, and they are life" (Jo 6:63). In the same conversation, Peter acknowledged what Jesus said, and told Jesus, "You have the words of eternal life" (v. 68). God's words, either spoken by Jesus or written in the Bible, have life. The author of Hebrews says, "For the word of God is living" (He 4:12). God's words give life to those who read and study the Scriptures.

When you get the life of God in you, that's the foundation for faith. If you have God's life in your heart, you can trust Him and live as He requires.

But let me quickly add, just knowing the Bible doesn't automatically give you faith. The Pharisees of Jesus' day knew the Bible well. They knew the content of Scripture and they knew the exact words of Scripture, but they rejected Jesus and contributed to His crucifixion. I have met many church members who knew the Bible well, but were not men or women of faith. Faith is *believing* what you read in the Bible and *acting* on what you know. I've never seen a person of faith who didn't know the Bible and attempt to live by its message.

Which brings me to the fourth point: Act on what you know. In other words, *your faith grows by constant exercise.* Act on the Bible's instructions. When the Bible says to repent, a person of faith turns from sin. When the Bible says to serve God, a person of faith begins immediately to minister. Notice Paul described the "work of faith" (1 Th 1:3) in the Thessalonian believers. They "became examples to all in Macedonia," the state in which they lived (v. 7). From them, "the word of the Lord has sounded forth" (v. 8).

Just as you get stronger muscles by exercise, you get stronger faith by spiritual exercise. The more you exercise, the stronger you get. You don't get stronger reading about exercising, thinking about exercising, or even watching exercise videos. You must exercise to get stronger, and do it regularly. Push your Christian life beyond the normal limits of your expectation. The more times you take a step of faith, the easier it will become.

Therefore, to have growing faith, you must know the Bible and apply it to your life. Don't wait for God to drop it on you. You must seize it by faith. Begin studying the Bible in a big way to learn everything you can about the bigness of God. Next, apply what you learn from the Bible. Because the Lord is a big God, who does big things, you should begin doing bigger things for God than you're doing now. The bigger the things you attempt for God, the bigger your faith can grow. Push your faith beyond your expectations. Attempt something bigger than you've ever done in your life. If you fail, start over again. If you succeed, you'll grow and become stronger.

When the Bible says, "The just shall live by faith" (Ro 1:17), it means they live by the Bible and apply it to their life every day. You start with the "milk of the word" (1 Pe 2:2), then go on to the "meat of the word" (He 5:12–14). You start with basic exercises, then go on to more difficult things. You toddle before you walk, and you walk before you run. In faith, you begin by removing small stones in your shoes, then move rocks in the path of life. As you grow, you'll eventually move mountains (see Mk 11:23).

Experiencing Faith

Make a promise to God. I said I read the Bible through each year. That's what I want you to do. Would you promise God in prayer right now you'll read it through in one year? Write the following in your journal as you pray, "Lord, I will read through the Bible this year."

Begin today. Look in the Appendix to see today's daily Bible reading, and begin today.

Memorize the following Bible verses: Matthew 17:20, 21:22; John 14:13; Romans 1:17, 10:17; James 5:17–18.

Revisit your dream statement, developed in Day 5. Write down the biggest thing you want God to do for you. Compare your dream to the four steps I gave in today's lesson. Is your dream something God wants for you? If so, begin praying for it in an aggressive way. "If you can believe, all things are possible to him who believes" (Mk 9:23).

Suggested Reading: John 6:61–71

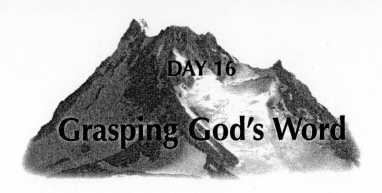

DAY 16

Grasping God's Word

> "But shun profane and vain babblings: for they will increase unto more ungodliness."
>
> (2 Ti 2:16, KJV)

Previously, I have suggested you read and study the Bible every day. But I haven't given you any guidelines to study the Bible. Today I would like to give you some practical "handles" to get hold of Scripture. I didn't choose the word *handle* aimlessly. It was a phrase I heard as a young Christian at Baptist Bible College. I don't remember if it was a Bible class lecture or a chapel speaker, but I remember the young speaker saying, "You must grab the Bible as you would grab a sword or a hammer."

The speaker said the Bible was our tool, just as a sword was the tool of a soldier. "And take . . . the sword of the Spirit, which is the word of God" (Ep 6:17). He mentioned you must grab the sword of Scriptures tightly, or the enemy could knock it out of your hand.

The speaker was a young man who had ministered among servicemen in the military, and I admired his snappy dress and forceful language. He held his Bible tightly with all five fingers and challenged one student sitting in the front row to pull the Bible from his hand using two fingers. Obviously, the student couldn't do it.

"There are five ways to grasp tightly the Bible, just as we have five fingers," the young speaker told the audience. "Use these five ways to learn the Bible, and no one can jerk it from your heart."

After you read today's chapter, I want you to use five "fingers" to grasp tightly the Word of God so no one can pry it out of your heart's fingers.

Five Ways to Grasp Scripture

First, you need to *hear the Word of God*. As the young man explained, the primary means to hear is to attend church to hear the Word of God preached. This means you need to listen to the exhortation from Scripture. It also includes hearing the Bible taught in Bible study, hearing the Word explained.

Preaching and teaching are similar in that they both use Scripture, and at times some preaching explains the Bible and some teaching is motivational. Preaching and teaching have soft edges, so they merge into one another, but they have hard cores. Preaching uses the Word to motivate for proper living, and teaching explains the Word for proper understanding.

How should you listen to Scripture? As attentively as a crying little girl listens to her mother console her. As carefully as a soldier listens to commands for battle because his life is at stake. As carefully as a student listens to a teacher explain a test. You should listen to God's Word because He tells us in Scripture how to live.

Second, Christians are told to *read God's Word*. Paul told Timothy, "Give attention to reading" (1 Ti 4:13). God has promised "Blessed is he who reads" (Re 1:3). Since the words "to bless" means "to add value," when you read the Scriptures daily, you're adding the value of enjoyment and growth to your life.

You ought to read daily because you have daily needs. You ought to read *expectantly* because God promises to reveal Himself through the Word. You ought to read every book in the Bible because all Scripture is about God, and if you miss one section, you won't know everything you can about God.

Reading is so important. James tells us to be "swift to hear" (Jam 1:19). We are told, "He who has an ear, let him hear" (Re 2:7). Why? Because Jesus said, "If anyone hears My voice and opens the door, I will come in to him" (Re 3:20).

More than a hundred years ago a seminary student was impressed with the Bible teaching of D. L. Moody. When the student was asked if he read the Bible, he said, "No."

"What do you read in seminary?" Mr. Moody asked.

"Books to explain the Bible," was the young student's reply.

"I suggest you read the Bible all the way through to find out what it says." The student went on to become one of the great Bible teachers of America.

You may listen to sermons and Christian music; you may even see religious presentations in movies and on TV, but you won't really know what the Bible says until you read it for yourself.

The third point the young man said was to *study Scriptures.* This means you must dig into Scriptures, comparing Scriptures to Scriptures (see 1 Co 2:13). You study the Scriptures to see what they mean, then you study to apply them to your personal life. Keep these two steps of study apart. Study first to interpret Scriptures. This is where you determine what the Bible means. Second, apply the Bible to your life by asking, "What does it mean to me?"

When Paul went to the city of Berea, he found a group of people who were not willing to accept what he said until they could prove it in Scriptures. "These [believers in Berea] were more noble . . . in that they received the word with all readiness of mind, and searched the scriptures daily, whether those things were so" (Ac 17:11, KJV).

These Christians were noble, which means they were sincere believers who wanted to know the truth. Is that a picture of you? Daily they searched the Scriptures to determine if Paul was telling the truth. The word *searched* means "to sift," as kernels of grain are sifted to separate every single piece of good grain from its chaff or husk. Likewise, we study the Word of God by examining every word in Scripture.

Remember Peter asked the Lord, "Lord, to whom shall we go? You have the words of eternal life" (Jo 6:68).

The fourth way to grasp the Bible is to *memorize the Word.* As a young believer I began memorizing Bible verses. No one had to tell me to do it. I was like a blind man seeing for the first time, and I wanted to remember everything I saw. I was like a thirsty man drinking for the first time the water of eternal life, and I didn't want to forget how it tasted.

The psalmist teaches, "Your word I have hidden in my heart, that I might not sin against You" (Ps 119:11). He is telling us to do more than memorize the facts of our faith. He knew the Word of God in our hearts will help keep us from sin. It will keep us close to God.

You should also memorize the Scriptures so you will know what God expects of you. Then the Bible will help you obey His commandments. "Remember all the commandments of the Lord and do them" (Nu 15:39).

The last way to grasp the Bible is to *meditate on Scripture.* God told Joshua at the beginning of his leadership, "This Book of the Law shall not depart from your mouth, but you shall meditate in it day and night" (Jos 1:8).

Meditating on the Bible is thinking about it. You think what God is saying about Himself, and you think to apply the Bible to your life. God told Joshua that meditation would make him successful, "Then you will make your way prosperous, and then you will have good success" (Jos 1:8).

Why will meditation guarantee spiritual success? Because you will probably become like the things you dream about and what you yearn to be, "As he thinks in his heart, so is he" (Pr 23:7).

At the end of his lecture, the military-type young man again handed his Bible to a teenage boy on the front row and told him to hold the Bible with two fingers. "See if you have enough strength in two fingers to keep me from pulling this Bible from you."

The teenager grasped the Bible tightly with his thumb and forefinger, but the speaker easily pulled the Bible away. Then he said,

"If you only use two fingers—to listen and read—you don't have a firm grip on the Bible." Then the speaker commented, "I can pull the Bible from you because I have all five fingers firmly on the Bible."

I never forgot that graphic lesson. I had to do more than attend church and listen to sermons and read my Bible daily. I had to hear . . . read . . . study . . . memorize . . . and meditate. More than anything else, I believe the Bible is foundational to my faith, and I have been able to get great things from God because I've attempted to let the Bible have a great influence in my life.

Experiencing Faith

How can you learn more of God's Word so you will know Him better and obey Him more fully? First, *make a commitment to attend meetings* where you can listen to preaching and teaching of the Word of God. Obviously the first and most important thing is to regularly attend a Bible-teaching church. Also, when great men or women of God visit your area, go hear them. I believe in the "hot poker" approach to getting great dreams from God. When the poker is put into the fire, it becomes hot. You'll get more faith by listening to men and women of faith.

Second, *recommit yourself to a planned schedule of reading and studying the Bible.*

Third, *memorize Scriptures* that will reinforce these lessons. Begin today to memorize one of these three verses that we've just read (Jos 1:8; Ps 119:11; Ac 17:11).

Finally, *type or write the above three verses on a card or paper to review several times today.* Keep them handy in a pocket or purse, or tape them on your refrigerator door or in your workstation. Review them during breaks at work or when you have a few free moments throughout the day. Review often with a view of both memorizing and meditating on each verse.

Suggested Reading: Psalm 119:1–16

DAY 17

Conversion Is Just the Beginning

> "Therefore, if anyone is in Christ, he is a new creation; old things have passed away; behold, all things have become new."
>
> (2 Co 5:17)

If you've been doing the assignments at the end of each day's reading, you've probably experienced some spiritual growing pains. That ought to give some assurance that you have received the life of God. In this chapter, we'll look at some of the reasons that I knew I was born again. Then I'll ask the question, "Do you know that you have the life of God within?"

We all have doubts. But if we focus on our doubts, they will always unnerve us. Focus on who God is, and on what He is doing today in your heart. My favorite verse is Philippians 1:6, "Being confident of this very thing, that He who has begun a good work in you will complete it until the day of Jesus Christ."

Everything Was New

On that cold winter night of my conversion, I got up off my knees and stood beside Pastor Donnelson as he introduced me to the congregation. He told them I had been born again and they were my new spiritual family. I then walked slowly among them, accepting their welcome and feeling their arms around me. I thought I would never reach the door through that gauntlet of happy huggers.

115

"Praise the Lord, Brother Jerry," an old man exclaimed as he almost squeezed the life out of me.

"Amen," echoed a tiny wrinkled woman whose eyes were filled with tears.

I was 18 years old. During my last years at Brookville High School and my first two years at Lynchburg College I seldom went inside a church. I liked pretty girls, fast cars, late-night parties with the Wall Gang, sandlot baseball, a hard-fought football scrimmage, poker games, and beer busts. But I was about to leave that behind. My new friends at Park Avenue Baptist Church had witnessed my new birth and were welcoming me into the kingdom of God. It was the beginning of my new life among them.

I learned later that as Jim Moon and I entered the church that night, those people began to pray silently for our salvation. A few of them recognized me as the rowdy Falwell kid from Rustburg Road, whose father ran booze during the Depression. From the moment I walked up the aisle into their fellowship and took my seat in the front row, those who knew me, and even those who didn't, were praying that God would speak to me through Pastor Donnelson's sermon.

When that old white-haired stranger leaned forward to invite me to kneel with him at the altar, they were all leaning forward with him. And when he knelt beside me, opened his Bible, and began to present God's plan of salvation, those dear people surrounded us with their prayers. That night, January 20, 1952, as I accepted Christ as my Savior, almost every one of them sat patiently on the cold metal folding chairs, their heads bowed, their eyes closed, and their lips moving in silent prayer on my behalf until God's business in my life had been accomplished. Evangelism in that church was teamwork, and almost no one left the room until the work of God was finished.

I had no idea of what was about to happen to me that moment at the back door of the little two-story cement-block church in Lynchburg. Upstairs in the warmth of that congregation, I had accepted Jesus as my Savior, but on the icy cold sidewalk just minutes later I met the youth pastor, Jack Dinsbeer, who would introduce me to Jesus as my Lord.

"What happened to you tonight," Jack said, "is just a beginning. Don't let your new faith shrivel up before it has a chance to grow."

His words sounded strange and ominous. "Don't let your new faith shrivel up." There was so much about the spiritual life that I didn't understand. Everything was new to me. I had been born again. Wasn't that enough? I had seen the instant wonderful change in my father at his deathbed conversion. I supposed that the altar experience was the end of it for me. But I was wrong.

Conversion is just the beginning.

Those who receive Jesus Christ are born again. It is the start of your life with Christ. "But as many as received Him . . . were born . . . of God" (Jo 1:12–13). Let me ask you, "Have you been born again?"

Nicodemus was a religious ruler who came to Jesus by night. He tried to flatter Jesus by telling Him, "We know that You are a teacher come from God; for no one can do these signs that You do unless God is with him" (Jo 3:2). Jesus answered Nicodemus, "Unless one is born again, he cannot see the kingdom of God" (v. 3). Religious people have to be born again, and so do terrible sinners.

In the Garden of Eden, God told Adam he could eat the fruit from any tree in the Garden except "the tree of the knowledge of good and evil . . . for in the day that you eat of it you shall surely die" (Ge 2:17). Adam ate the fruit and died. But he didn't immediately die physically. "So all the days that Adam lived were nine hundred and thirty years; and he died" (Ge 5:5). What died immediately when Adam sinned? His soul died! The Bible describes this as being "dead in trespasses and sins" (Ep 2:1).

Jesus told Nicodemus, "You must be born again" because he—like us—was spiritually dead.

New Desires

When you are born again, you receive a new nature. This means you have new desires to serve God and fellowship with Him. Before I was born again, I didn't want to go to church. As a boy, my mother had taken me to Sunday school, but when I got old enough, I quit going to Sunday school and church. When I was born again, I wanted to obey God and hear the Word of God preached. I wanted to go to church. God said, "Everyone who loves God will love others who love God, because they are all born again by the same Lord" (1 Jo 5:1, *My Translation*).

After salvation I wanted to read my Bible, because the Bible is "the testimony: that God has given us eternal life" (1 Jo 5:11). I had hundreds of questions I asked the youth pastor of Park Avenue Baptist Church. I knew I was born again because my experience was different. The very next week, I bought my first Bible and began reading it hungrily. I memorized whole chapters in the Bible.

I had a new desire to pray to God. When I was young, Mother taught me prayers and I prayed them as a child. When I got old enough, I quit my regular prayers. When I got into trouble, I called out to God, but that was not like talking to God because I didn't love Him or know Him. I called out to Him because I was scared or needed something. But after I was born again, I found myself talking to God on a regular basis. I slowly began learning how to have a daily prayer time. I knew I was saved because I began experiencing the wonderful blessings of prayer.

Some people accept Christ as Savior, then later have doubts. I'll admit that I always had doubts about God before I was born again. But when I accepted Jesus Christ as my Savior, my major doubts were gone. I had a confidence about spiritual things. "When you believe on the Son of God, you will know that you have eternal life" (1 Jo 5:13, *My Translation*).

When I was born again, I received a great desire to share my new faith with my friends in the Wall Gang. These were boys from the Fairview Heights section of Lynchburg, Virginia. We usually gathered at the Pickeral Café and sat on a wall next to the store. Some people are afraid to tell their family and friends that they have been born again. Maybe these Christians are afraid of ridicule or ostracism. I wasn't afraid of what my gang would say, not at all. I was afraid I couldn't explain what happened to me, or I would mess up my testimony and turn them against God. I wanted to share with them what God had done for me. Conversion was the greatest experience of my life, and I wanted them to have what I had. I believed God could save every one of them, just as He had saved me. No one had to motivate me to witness to my friends. It was more than natural; it was what I wanted to do. I knew I was born again because I had a great desire to tell everyone what happened to me. Most of the Wall Gang eventually met Christ as I did.

After I prayed to receive Jesus, I didn't have much of a struggle to quit my former sins. I just loved God so much that I didn't want to get involved in those things again. Don't get me wrong, I'm not claiming to be sinlessly perfect. And I'm not claiming that I was never again tempted by the world. As a young Christian, there were a lot of things I didn't know, and there were a lot of things I didn't do properly. Like a baby, I was learning to walk, and babies fall down a lot. But I experienced the truth of 1 John 5:4, "Whatever is born of God overcomes the world. And this is the victory that has overcome the world—our faith." I knew I was born again because I experienced a new desire to please God all the time and a new desire to change my former evil ways.

In this chapter, I've described some of the new things that happened to me when I was born again. But let me remind you that the born-again experience is to have Jesus Christ—a person—living in your life. "He who has the Son has life; he who does not have the Son of God does not have life" (1 Jo 5:12).

Experiencing Faith

Today I want you to *do a checkup on your spiritual health.* Let's find out where you are with your experiences in Christ.

My Experiences as a Christian	Strong Confidence	Mild Desires	No Experience	The Opposite Feelings
I have new spiritual desires to know God.				
I have new desires to learn the Scriptures.				
I have new desires to talk to God in prayer.				
I have a new burden to see my friends know God.				
I have a new desire to worship with Christians.				
I have a new desire to overcome sin (old habits).				

Focus prayer on your weaknesses. If you are weak in one of the above areas, make it a matter of prayer. Prayer moves God on your behalf, but it also changes you. When you begin praying for an area, you will begin to experience God's work in your heart. Ask God to transform you in each area.

Suggested Reading: John 3

DAY 18

Discerning Faith

"Be filled with the Spirit."

(Ep 5:18)

God knows that you need to be stretched to grow your faith, so God will send unique individuals to stretch you. I've learned over the years that individuals who teach and mentor us stretch us according to their strengths. They probably stretch us the way they were stretched. My college president, Beauchamp Vick, stretched me to be a leader. My Springfield, Missouri, pastor stretched me with pastoral skills and passion, and my youth pastor, Jack Dinsbeer, stretched me with Bible skills. Of course, interacting with sinful human people can also stretch us as their sins and weaknesses rub against our weaknesses and grow our character.

In today's lesson I want to stretch you with some deeper-life attitudes and passions that I learned early in my ministry. Notice that the two people I describe in this lesson didn't teach me soulwinning, nor did they stretch me with the Great Commission. God used these people to give me what I needed at the time I needed it. I needed to ground my faith deeply in God.

Going Deeper

How often God sends men or women our way just at the right time to help us when we need it. It was a woman and her father who helped introduce me to the deeper spiritual life. When Ann Whittemore and her father, R. B. Whittemore, walked into Thomas Road Baptist Church in the early days of my ministry, I immediately noticed their dignity. They had a spiritual maturity about them. Ann Whittemore was tall, twenty-five, unmarried, and a very spiritual person. Her father was a successful businessman from St. Louis, Missouri, a widower who had retired in his mid-fifties to a 750-acre ranch in southern Virginia, about twenty-five miles from Lynchburg.

In the early days of my ministry, I often drove down to their farm for fellowship and spiritual stimulation. God was speaking to me during those times of conversation with the Whittemores.

Mr. Whittemore told me, "God doesn't want you to achieve great things in His name, Jerry. He just wants you to love Him, to trust Him, to wait upon Him, and to praise Him. Then He can achieve what He desires through you!"

I always drove away from the Whittemores feeling spiritually fed. Don't misunderstand. Being with them wasn't easy. Mr. Whittemore made me examine myself deeply, and he raised the bar spiritually. I went back many times to learn from them.

The Whittemores knew how hard I worked to build Thomas Road Baptist Church, so Mr. Whittemore said to me time and time again, "Be sure, Jerry, that your inner spiritual life keeps up with all the tasks that you have appointed for yourself. Be sure you stay close to the Father as you rush about doing your Father's business." The Whittemores taught me that God would attend to the breadth of my ministry if I would attend to its depth.

When I left the Whittemores, I usually raced back to make a few important calls because I had spent a whole day with them away from the office. When I went to visit them, I didn't complete my goal of a hundred house calls a day. When I got home, I always had a list of telephone messages, a pile of letters, or a trustee meeting to attend.

When I drove fastest, Mr. Whittemore's words would always echo in my mind: "Be sure you stay close to the Father as you rush about doing your Father's business." I began to pray as I drove. My car became a chapel, my dashboard an altar of worship. God was beginning to do something special in my life, and I could feel Him doing it.

The inward journey—that personal spiritual quest to know God better and to give His Spirit complete control in our lives—begins the moment of our conversion. But for many of us there is another time in our lives that we can look back on as marking another type of beginning. One evening after visiting the Whittemores was a time of beginning for me.

As my car neared Lynchburg, I turned left onto the road that leads down to Timberlake and parked my car in a clearing by the water. The sky was streaked with deep purple, amber, and violet. The sunset made a gold path across the lake. I walked down to the water's edge and skipped a flat stone across the surface.

"Slow me down, Lord," I prayed. "The Whittemores are right. You don't need me to break my neck building a church. You need me just to love You."

Late that afternoon I walked beside the lake and thought about Jesus walking beside the Sea of Galilee almost two thousand years ago. He too needed time to praise His Father in heaven. He too needed to get away from the day's rush and listen to the still small voice of God speaking in His heart. And if Jesus Himself spent so much time and energy during His short ministry on this earth in fellowship with His heavenly Father, then how much more I needed it.

Then I remembered a little book that the Whittemores had given me as I rushed away that day. I returned to my car, unwrapped the package, and opened the small tan-covered book with a single rose etched on its cover above the title, *Waiting on God*. The book's author was Andrew Murray, one of those "deeper spiritual life" advocates that the Whittemores often quoted. Inside the book was a series of thirty short devotional messages, one for each day of the month. Apparently God had given Andrew Murray the friendship of Mr. and Mrs. Albert A. Head, who had blessed him with "a bright home" and "days of quiet waiting," just as God had led the Whittemores to me.

Early in 1958, the Whittemores gave me the first English edition of Watchman Nee's *The Normal Christian Life*. Like Andrew Murray, Nee opened up the world of the Spirit to me.

"A forgiven sinner," Nee writes, "is quite different from an ordinary sinner, and a consecrated Christian is quite different from an ordinary Christian. . . . If we yield wholly to Him and claim the power of His indwelling Spirit, we need wait for no special feelings or supernatural manifestations, but can simply look up and praise Him that something has already happened. We can confidently thank Him that the glory of God has already filled His temple. 'Know ye not that your body is a temple of the Holy Ghost which is in you, which ye have of God.'"[1]

With Watchman Nee I learned to celebrate and to practice the presence of the Holy Spirit every day. I know deeply spiritual Christians who differ with one another on eschatology, church polity, or other non-essentials, yet I have never met a Christian who lived a powerful and productive life who didn't credit everything to the presence of the Holy Spirit living and working in and through his or her life.

I believed then, as I believe now, that there are two sides to this deeper spiritual life issue. Waiting upon the Lord, as Andrew Murray recommends, is just one side to consider. The other truth we must not forget is that we can wait forever and never really do anything for God or the church. I believe in equal doses of work and waiting. The deeper spiritual life demands action, and productive action requires the deeper spiritual life.

During those first five years at Thomas Road, I tried to find some balance between my urge to win the world single-handedly and my deep desire to grow spiritually. The struggle between those two worlds went on within me every day. Little by little, I learned how to incorporate both worlds into my life: the practical world of action and the continuous fellowship with my Lord. And little by little I felt a calmness settle over me that can only be attributed to the presence and inward control of God's Holy Spirit in my life. All that was settled early in my ministry, thanks to the Whittemores and those great men and women of the deeper spiritual life whose writings helped to focus my life. I was beginning to learn how to be both "spiritual" and "natural" in a way that allowed me to enter into His rest and truly enjoy the Christian life.

The Spirit's Filling

To get this spiritual life, Paul writes, "Be filled with the Spirit" (Ep 5:18). You get the Spirit's filling just as you get filled physically drinking a glass of water. First you realize you're thirsty. That's what the Whittemores did for me; they made me thirst for more of the Holy Spirit. Second, you pick up the glass, expecting to have your thirst quenched. This is the faith part. You must expect God to keep His Word to fill your life when you do your part. Third, you simply drink. I would suggest you drink by praying, "Lord, fill my life with the Holy Spirit."

If you are a believer, you already have the Holy Spirit in your heart. You don't have to get more of the Holy Spirit, He has to get more of you.

The Holy Spirit will do what you ask, because God keeps His promise. So the fourth thing is to yield to His control. Now that the Holy Spirit is filling you, let Him do His will in you. If He points out bad habits or unsavory words in your vocabulary, quit them.

The Holy Spirit has come into your life to make you *holy*, so you must sweep out the dirt. I realize you may have a difficult time getting rid of certain habits because they are ingrained in your life. The Holy Spirit has power to help you. That's why He entered your life.

There are many other things the Holy Spirit will do for you. He will illuminate Scriptures so you'll understand things in the Bible you've never seen. He'll lead you to people for witness or ministry. He'll give you a new love for others, especially those you haven't been able to love. He'll make you more generous with your money for charitable needs. And if you've had difficulty with self-control, He'll give you resolution and discipline.

The Holy Spirit comes into your life to help you do the will of God. Some call this the "Spirit-directed life" or the "Spirit-filled life." There are a lot of other phrases to describe this experience of walking with God. I know many church people disagree with other church people over their unique doctrine of what the Holy Spirit does for a Christian. They may have different theological titles for this experience, but most of them have the same experience. I've heard people call it the "deeper Christian life," but I like Watchman Nee's term the *normal Christian life*. If you let the Holy Spirit control your life, you can do more for God and be more for God. That's what normal Christians should do.

Experiencing Faith

It's hard to assign someone to be filled with the Spirit, but that's what I want you to do. I want you to pray and **ask the Holy Spirit to fill you with Himself**. It's as simple as asking your server for a refill of coffee or water. When you see your cup is empty and you want more, simply ask. "How much more will your heavenly Father give the Holy Spirit to those who ask Him!" (Lk 11:13).

Pray, "Lord, fill me with the Holy Spirit now."

Sometimes the Father can't fill us with the Holy Spirit because we've got sin in our lives. The Spirit is holy, so He is silenced. If your hands are dirty and you get dirt on your glass, the server doesn't want to fill a dirty glass. It needs washing.

You need to learn again the lesson of confession and forgiveness. "If we confess our sins, He is faithful and just to forgive us our sins and to cleanse us from all unrighteousness" (1 Jo 1:9). So let's get the glass clean so we can be filled with the Spirit.

Pray, "Lord, forgive me of my sin by the blood of Jesus. I'm sorry for displeasing You. Cleanse me and make me clean."

Sometimes the Lord doesn't fill us because we aren't glorifying

Him and ministering for Him. We are not actively trying to serve God.

Pray, "Lord, rekindle my *life purpose* and use me to serve You this day. Help me refocus on my *life plan* for this day. Now fill me with the Holy Spirit to do what I'm supposed to do this day."

Suggested Reading: John 7:32–39

DAY 19

Making Faith Statements

"Jesus told His disciples: 'Have faith in God! If you have faith in God and don't doubt, you can tell this mountain to get up and jump into the sea, and it will.'"

(Mk 11:22–23, *My Translation*)

There is more than one way to express faith, just as there is more than one way to express love to a family member. As you express love by an embrace, giving a gift, or spending time with the one you love, so you express faith by obeying, serving, or trusting God for an answer before it comes.

Today's lesson focuses on making a faith statement to God for something in prayer before you get the answer. You do this by telling others what you seek or by asking God for your request. I did this once by announcing to the church that a student was going to recover from an accident when everyone thought he would die.

We must be very careful that what we announce is what God wants and not what we want. It's very easy to substitute our personal desires in place of God's desires. I've seen some well-meaning—but misguided—people claim answers to prayer that didn't come about. So, today's lesson will give some guidelines for making *faith statements* in prayer.

Claiming God's Healing

One of the greatest answers to prayer regarding healing came when I asked all the people of Thomas Road Baptist Church and Liberty University® to pray that God would heal Charles Hughes. His healing commanded more prayer attention and fasting than any other answer to prayer that I had seen up to that time. His healing convinced me God could do even more miraculous things in the future.

Charles Hughes was an upperclassman at Liberty University® who was called to evangelism. He was one of the most outstanding young men we've ever had at Liberty because the power of God was upon him to lead multitudes to Christ. He had preached in many of the largest churches in America while he was in his early twenties.

Charles was traveling to an evangelistic crusade in Harrisburg, Pennsylvania, in 1978 when the van in which he was riding was mangled in an accident with an eighteen-wheeler truck. Charles' head was crushed, and doctors removed the top of his skull because of swelling.

After doing everything possible, the doctors told us Charles would die. They asked if the family wanted to sign papers to donate his organs to living recipients. The medical community felt Charles was as good as dead.

I was preaching in Holland, Michigan, when the accident happened. I immediately flew to be with the family in York, Pennsylvania. His father, Robert Hughes, asked for me to call a day of fasting and prayer throughout the entire ministry. Some advised me not to do it because Charles was as good as dead and we'd be embarrassed.

I announced to everyone that Charles would live if we sincerely fasted and prayed from the depths of our hearts. I was so sure that God would answer our prayers that I announced to Thomas Road Baptist Church that Charles was going to speak at Liberty's graduation that year. Again, some told me I was foolhardy because graduation was only five months away and Charles was hanging onto a faint sliver of life.

Sometimes God gives an inner assurance—supernatural faith— that He is about to do something. As I prayed, I felt God was going to heal Charles. My feelings were an inner conviction, so much so, that I thanked God for his healing long before it happened. The Bible calls this "the prayer of faith" (Jam 5:15). This is when faith is absolutely sure the answer will come before it happens.

I've had this feeling of assurance—the prayer of faith—in my life on several occasions, especially when asking for money. However, don't get me wrong, and don't put me on a pedestal; there are times I have asked and didn't get what I asked.

Charles lived and was restored enough to bring a powerful message at the 1978 graduation. He wasn't as fluent as in his past sermons, but Charles was alive and the event was electric. God honored the faith of the entire Thomas Road Baptist Church family and Liberty student body. Today, Charles has gone on to earn his bachelor's, master's, and doctorate, and he works in our ministry.

Making Faith Statements

Let me give you some guiding principles on how to express your faith, because I don't want you to think you can get anything you "claim" in prayer. First, *your prayer statement must agree with Scripture.* God will do what He promised in Scripture; but you must be careful not to promise something that God has not promised. Jesus tells us, "If you abide in Me, and My words abide in you, you will ask what you desire, and it shall be done for you" (Jo 15:7). Of course, it is not always God's will to heal everyone. If he did, no one would ever die. But, when it is God's will to heal "nothing is too hard for the Lord."

According to this verse, there are three things that get prayers answered: (1) you must be abiding in Jesus, which means you have yielded yourself to Him, (2) God's Word must control your thinking and asking, and (3) you must ask to receive. Therefore, your prayers will be answered when you ask for things promised by the Bible. The problem is many people ask for selfish things and become skeptical when God doesn't answer them.

Second, you must *tie your faith statement to fasting and continual prayer.* Jesus said, "If you have faith . . . you will say to this mountain 'Move from here to there,' and it will move. . . . However, this kind does not go out except by prayer and fasting" (Ma 17:20–21). Can you really expect God to respond if you don't invest much time and sincerity in prayer? Just making a bold statement doesn't move mountains. So what must you do? You must make bold *faith statements* that come from every part of your being. Then you pray with all your heart, giving up sleep for an all-night prayer meeting. You fast and pray for a day, or for a week. You sacrifice everything because you know God can answer, and you keep praying until God *does* answer.

A casual request rolling off your tongue doesn't move God, but God responds when you pray so diligently that you cry and weep. So let me ask, when's the last time you've begged God for something?

Third, *because you know God can answer, you never give up.* You keep praying even when everything seems black, unless and until God has answered or given you a clear no. We prayed for Charles for fourteen weeks before he regained consciousness. The top of his skull remained off to allow the swelling to go down. A strong, bold *faith statement* is not something you pray once and forget about. No! When your faith tells you that the answer will come, you can't quit. You ask for it when you get up in the morning and when you pray at a meal. You ask for it while driving around your city, and you ask for it right before you pillow your head at night. You keep praying, because you believe in a personal God who is guiding you and whose promises are true.

The fourth principle is *don't doubt in the dark what God has shown you in the light.* Jesus said a condition for answers is to "not doubt in his heart . . . he will have whatever he says" (Mk 11:23). You can't work up confidence that God will answer. Neither does lasting confidence come from circumstances. When you have confidence God will answer, it comes from God.

In the fifth place, you must *have confidence your prayers are based on God's will.* "This is confidence . . . that if we ask according to His will He hears us, and we know when He hears us, we have the answers we seek of Him" (1 Jo 5:14–15, *My Translation*). You find God's will in God's Word. Sometimes it is God's will that a person dies; at other times it is not God's will for you to succeed in a project. Sometimes God wants you to fail so He can lead you in another direction. Paul prayed three times for healing or the removal of some sort of unnamed problem, but didn't get it (2 Co 12:7–10).

Sometimes you don't get your request because you haven't followed the biblical principle that leads to bold faith praying. You haven't prayed with others, you haven't allowed the Bible to control your life, or you haven't sacrificed your time, food, and sleep. You have not fasted. However, never forget you can make a difference when God leads you to make a bold *faith statement* that moves Him to an answer. When God puts a spirit of confidence in your heart, you can ask boldly in faith.

Experiencing Faith

For today's faith-building exercise, do three things. First, *make a list in your journal of past times you've had great confidence God would answer* as you prayed. Maybe someone else—your pastor or a friend or relative—had great faith and you joined in prayer for the answer. Maybe your faith grew as your faith connected with the faith of someone else. By writing down past successful experiences, you'll develop your faith to trust God for today.

Second, *write down the one thing you're most concerned about at present.* If you have faith to tell others about this request, write down the reasons you're confident the answer will come.

However, maybe you don't have confidence about the thing that presently concerns you. If you have doubts, write why you have doubts. Maybe getting your doubts on paper will help you see the situation objectively, then you'll know whether to make a positive *faith statement* or whether you shouldn't.

Third, *look to the future.* Look at the far-off future and the coming-week future. Make a list of some big things that will focus your prayer. These big requests may be personal issues in your life, or they could be big requests for your church or a Christian group that you associate with. Once these are listed, begin asking God to show you His will for these requests. Then ask God to give you faith to believe for a great answer.

When you can't make a *faith statement,* pray like the father of the boy who wasn't healed by the disciples, "Lord, I believe; help my unbelief!" (Mk 9:24). Maybe the Lord will hear your confession of unbelief and request for faith to give you faith. Then maybe the Lord will answer, as He did heal the boy (vv. 25–29).

Suggested Reading: Mark 11:12–26

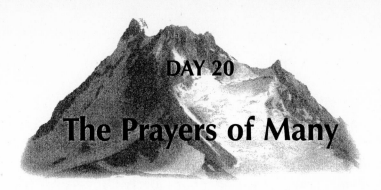

DAY 20

The Prayers of Many

"And when they had prayed, the place where they were assembled together was shaken."

(Ac 4:31)

"If two of you agree on earth concerning anything that they ask, it will be done for them by My Father in heaven."

(Ma 18:19)

The Bible tells us to pray with others to get our requests answered. "If two of you agree . . . ask, it will be done" (Ma 18:19). My best prayer partner is Macel, my wife. Over the years I've had many prayer partners, some at Bible college, some with Thomas Road Baptist Church, some with Moral Majority, and some with Liberty University®. You will have different prayer partners, for different needs, at different times in your life.

When we were interested in buying the defunct Donald Duck bottling building on Thomas Road, Percy Hall and I had to agree on the price of our offer before we went into the realty office, and we agreed how high we'd go. Jesus said when two people go to the Father in prayer, they have to agree before He will answer.

Today's lesson tells how I asked more than five thousand people to agree and pray together for a gigantic answer to prayer. That developed the faith of the Liberty University® community, and I want this lesson to develop your faith to pray with another person for a great answer to prayer.

Getting Many to Pray

I was getting ready for Liberty University® chapel on April 24, 1985, when someone told me our dean of students had been diagnosed with terminal cancer. He was given six weeks to six months to live. I immediately knew we had to do something. Vernon Brewer was dean of students and vice president at Liberty University®, and he had been the very first graduate of Liberty. The students loved Vernon because of his fairness in enforcing rules and his deep love for them. I don't remember saying the following, but some who heard me have reminded me that I made a bold *faith statement.* "We can't let Vernon die," was my first remark. "We've got to pray him well."

Without making a detailed plan of action, I went straight to the student body in chapel and announced what we should do. That plan of action came out of my heart, not my head. I announced that everyone—faculty, staff, and students—should give themselves to a day of prayer and fasting for the healing of Vernon Brewer on the next day, April 25, 1985. I asked everyone to spend at least one hour in intercession for his healing, reminding them that Jesus had given only one indication how long we should pray: "Could you not watch with Me one hour?" (Ma 26:40).

I didn't want students praying just anywhere—of course they could and did—but I wanted them to make a statement of faith with their time and feet, just as I was making a statement. I spontaneously asked for someone to draw a chart of a large clock—a prayer clock—and for all five thousand students to sign up on that clock when they would pray. I wanted a time commitment from each one. I asked each student to go to the prayer chapel for his or her one-hour prayer vigil. The small prayer chapel was open throughout the day and night. Of course many students prayed at other times, in addition to praying at the college chapel. All classes set aside some time to pray. Some classes were canceled to provide an additional hour of prayer.

The food service and cafeteria were shut down on that day. An announcement was made that those who needed to eat because they were diabetic or had some other physical problems would find food on the serving counter. There was bread, sandwich spread, and drinks. The students were allowed to go into a nearby refrigerator for milk and other foods that were necessary. Since we treat food as medicine for the sick, we expected those with special dietary needs to eat.

Approximately 3,700 dorm students usually ate in the university cafeteria each day, and about 1,700 students lived off campus. But only about 50 showed up to eat that day. We did not get an exact number who fasted; the leaders estimated more than 5,000 students fasted and came to the prayer chapel to pray on that one day.

I wish I could say that God healed Vernon Brewer instantly; it didn't happen the way I wanted, but it did happen. First, the doctors opened his chest and took out a five-pound cancerous mass. Next they treated him with radiation, followed by several months of chemotherapy. Then to make matters even worse, a terrible accident happened. A needle missed his vein and the medication dripped into his arm and ran down on the inside of his skin into his wrist and hand. It ate the skin off his arm and hand from inside out. Vernon did not need these complications of added fever and terrible side effects. He had skin grafts and several surgeries to repair the hand, all the while battling cancer. So while the healing was not instantaneous—it took more than a year—nevertheless, it was miraculous. The doctors predicted Vernon would die, but he didn't. It is essential to remember that it is not always God's will to heal. But when it is, "nothing is too hard for the Lord."

Vernon Brewer remained our dean of students at Liberty University® for years. Today he runs World Help, a large Christian humanitarian ministry. Every time I see Vernon, I'm reminded of what the Bible promises, "The prayer of faith will save the sick" (Jam 5:15). The following are principles to guide you as you pray with other believers.

Guidelines for Praying with Another

Make sure the thing for which you pray is in the will of God. I've heard some people wrongly ask for things that were not God's will. How do I know they were wrong? The will of God is always in harmony with the laws of God. You can't pray to fly, because it's contrary to the laws of gravity for a human to flap his arms and fly. You can't pray that you will get away with your sin. Remember, the will of God is in harmony with the Word of God. Therefore, your prayers must correspond to Bible promises.

Understand that there is value in the volume of prayer. Jesus has promised, "If two of you agree on earth concerning anything that they ask, it will be done for them by My Father in heaven" (Ma 18:19). If two can get answers to prayer, think of what happens when thousands pray together. When two or more *agree*, it means they talk together, have faith together, and pray together. Just as many shoulders are needed to lift a car off an accident victim, it takes many people praying to move heaven and earth.

> The greater your obstacle or prayer request . . .
>
> * The more people are needed to pray.
> * The more often they must pray.
> * The longer they must pray.
> * The more intensely they must pray.

Pray with another person, because it will build your faith for bold praying. Our faith can grow from the faith of another person, especially when "two of you agree on earth concerning anything that they ask" (Ma 18:19). When we agree with another, we feel each other's confidence and strengthen each other's faith to pray for bigger things than we might otherwise ask.

Also, when we hear our prayers through the ears of another, we will control any desire to pray wrongly or to pray for the wrong thing. I've seen some get carried away with outlandish requests by "naming it" in prayer and "claiming it" from God. A sincere prayer partner will help us pray honestly. After all, to have great faith we must be honest before God.

We become honest when we pray with another, especially if it's our spouse. We can't claim false spirituality when praying with people who know us. We are more humble and exact when we know someone is praying the same words as our prayer.

But maybe faith is the greatest thing we get from our prayer partner. Another person's strong faith may lift our weakened faith. The other person's ability to intercede may teach us how to do it more effectively.

God hears when we pray with *sincerity and passion*. That happens when people give up their physical food to fast and pray, then they hunger and thirst after righteousness. Many students told me that they fasted for the first time when fasting for Vernon. Because of their youthful faith, sincerity, purity—and great passion—God heard and answered.

The faith of another person helps us know what God can do, and it motivates us to know Him personally. When you come with a great request and you have great faith in God, you honor God. It's then He delights to do something big for you. I honestly believed that God can heal and that God could heal Vernon, so the next logical step was to ask God to do it. And since I really believed it in my heart, I announced to the students to fast and pray for Vernon's healing. "But without faith it is impossible to please Him, for he who comes to God must believe that He is, and that He is a rewarder of those who diligently seek Him" (He 11:6). God was pleased by the vast amount of faith shown by many, and He healed Vernon Brewer in response.

Experiencing Faith

Record a big answer. Write in your journal a previous time(s) when you prayed with a special person or a special group. Why was that prayer time special to you? Also, what great answer(s) did you receive because you were praying with them? As you reflect on those special times in the past, it may motivate you to seek a partner or group in the future. Also, your reflection will tell you what type of experience or partners to seek in the future.

How was your faith strengthened? As you continue to reflect on past experiences, make a list in your journal of how your faith was strengthened by that particular partner or group. You might include the size of your answer to measure how your faith was strengthened.

List two or three prayer challenges. We all have challenges every day in every area of our lives. Write down these two or three items you believe God would have you target in prayer.

List a potential prayer partner. As you think of a special prayer challenge, think of those with whom you might like to pray. Why would you choose them? What strength could they add to your faith? How is God leading you to pray with them? Determine to contact them with a view of making an appointment to pray together.

Here are some hints to approach a prayer partner. Don't ask someone to pray with you until you determine if that person is interested in your prayer project. You might want to tell the burden you have for a specific prayer project. Give the person information why he or she should pray with you before asking for a commitment. Unless you are praying with your spouse or another family member, the person should be the same sex as you.

Tell your potential prayer partner what you've learned from this day's reading. When you share your desire to pray with the person and your burden for the prayer project, he or she will more likely agree to pray with you. Then, when "two of you agree . . . it will be done" (Ma 18:19).

Suggested Reading: Matthew 17:14–21

DAY 21

Extreme Conditions

> "But when you fast . . . your Father who sees in secret will reward you openly."
>
> (Ma 6:16, 18)

What should you do when you face a crisis so terrible there's nothing humanly possible you can do to solve it? Granted, sometimes you pray with all your might, then get off your knees to work diligently to solve the problem. But sometimes there seems to be nothing you can do to work your way out of a dilemma.

Sometimes it's a medical crisis and there's nothing doctors can do. Sometimes the crisis is a failing project or apparently irreconcilable human hatred. Remember, Esther and the nation fasted when faced with a Jewish holocaust. Samuel and the nation fasted when they found themselves in bondage to the Philistines. Moses fasted when he received the Ten Commandments, and Jesus fasted forty days as He prepared for His earthly ministry.

I fasted twice, forty days on each occasion, when I was faced with losing Liberty University®. If the university collapsed, I would have lost my most important contribution to the cause of Christ.

Your crisis may not be as financially severe as mine, but crises may be like beauty; they exist in the eye of the beholder. You may face a crisis just as severe as mine, because you may risk losing the things you've spent a lifetime building or the people who are most important to you. I want to teach you how to fast when that phone call comes or when that crisis hits.

Maybe you've got a problem that's not life threatening, but it's a lingering threat. Maybe you've got a junior-sized problem that, if it's not solved, could become your personal national disaster. I want you to read and live with me through my crisis, so you'll know what to do when your day of calamity strikes. Then look carefully at the principles to guide you to a solution. There is help for you, so don't miss a single sentence today.

My Greatest Crisis

In 1986 Liberty University® had more than five thousand students, and buildings and a campus worth $250 million without long-term debt. I had raised the money by direct appeal on television for whatever buildings or projects were needed. Also, we raised funds by direct mail. Raising cash was never difficult for me. Liberty was the fastest growing Christian school in the world, and we received more than $50 million in gifts every year. But when Jim Bakker and Jimmy Swaggart fell in 1987 and drew terrific media attention, it became clear by the late '80s that we could no longer raise money through television appeals and we could not support the university financially by direct mail. Because of the national religious scandals, the evangelical religious community would never be the same again.

I often compare television ministries to what happened in the savings and loan industry. When the bad ones began falling like dominos, many good savings and loans were wiped out in the tidal wave. Likewise, many strong evangelical media ministries like ours were permanently hurt. People stopped giving their money to all religious programs that were on television because of a credibility crunch. Contributions to *The Old Time Gospel Hour* and Liberty University® went down about $25 million a year. We had depended on that $25 million; it was in our budget.

Suddenly we found ourselves unable to raise money to pay bills.

Then, after four consecutive years of $25 million deficits, we had $110 million in liability debt. We had students on campus, and we had to educate them. We couldn't send them home.

The first thing I did was to dismantle the Moral Majority and get out of the political arena. I put all my emphasis back in Lynchburg and concentrated all my energies on Liberty University®. I went through days and nights of fasting and prayer . . . just to raise enough to pay our electric bill or meet salaries. (On one occasion the faculty went without pay because we didn't have any money. That's how dark things were, but to the credit of a wonderful faculty, not one of them resigned over the financial disruption.)

From 1991 to 1996 I practiced fasting and prayer as never before in my personal life. Survival was the name of the game. Finally, at the end of the fiscal year, June 30, 1996, by stringent budget cuts and selling off unneeded property, the debt had been reduced from $110 million to approximately $50 million.

Besides the financial debt, there was a double-barrel shotgun pointed at our head with both hammers cocked. Liberty University® was threatened with losing its regional accreditation because SACS (the Southern Association of Colleges and Schools) would not reaffirm the accreditation for a university that had such precarious indebtedness. We were notified that Liberty had to reduce its debt before it could continue its accredited status. SACS put Liberty on probation in December 1996. Without accreditation, I didn't think the University could continue. Without accreditation, we'd lose our students. With this crisis, I had to fast and fast seriously for money.

The summer of 1996 was time to do the unthinkable. I personally went on a forty-day fast. From July 20 to the first of September, I didn't eat anything, but only drank liquids. I was fasting and praying that 1997–98 would be the year when Liberty's debt burden would be removed. In that forty days I kept asking God for money, but I heard God say, "Jerry, don't look for My pocketbook, look for My heart."

God impressed upon my heart Jeremiah 29:13, "And you will seek Me and find Me, when you search for Me with all your heart." God impressed me to get close to Him, to listen to Him, and to trust Him. I found myself fasting to know God—a legitimate biblical principle—not fasting to get money. As I ended that forty-day fast, I was learning what God wanted to teach me. I didn't have a money answer, but I purposed to do everything humanly possible to prepare for an accreditation visit, knowing we could lose everything. Sometimes God doesn't give us more until we're ready to give up everything we have.

I ended my fast without a financial answer, and for the next twenty-five days I ate my regular meals. On the morning of September 25, 1996, as I was praying, God told me I could ask Him for money. Immediately I began a second forty-day fast. Many told me not to do it because of health reasons. For the next forty days I again fasted, taking only liquids. The first forty days had been a wonderful experience of spiritual communion with God. The second forty days were excruciating. I was extremely hungry at times, and I believe God was testing my resolve. I broke the fast forty days later. I had fasted eighty days out of one hundred and five days during the summer and fall and lost almost one hundred pounds.

Shortly after the fast was over, a courier walked into my office with a $27 million check to apply to long-term mortgage debt. Other private and corporate notes were assumed by outside interests. One individual has given Liberty University® close to $50 million since those two fasts. Second, the cash flow of Liberty University® was replenished with more than $2 million that gave us financial and institutional health. Third, God sent Liberty a new president, Dr. John Borek, a Ph.D. in Business Administration, who had been the Chief Financial Officer at Georgia State University. Without him we might not have been prepared for SACS' accreditation visit. Fourth, when SACS visited and evaluated Liberty, they removed all sanctions and recommended Liberty University® for ten more years of accreditation.

Steps Through a Crisis

The following are some spiritual principles that will help you fast when facing a crisis. *Make sure you are fasting for biblical purposes.* Examine your requests by the Word of God. I like the expression of the *New Living Translation*, "And even when you do ask, you don't get it because your whole motive is wrong—you want only what will give you pleasure" (Jam 4:3, NLT).

The secret to fasting is not giving up food, but *spending time in the presence of God.* Just going without food is only "good works," and God has never promised to bless legalism. Instead of pursuing food, you must pursue the presence of God. "When You said, 'Seek My face,' my heart said to You, 'Your face, Lord, I will seek'" (Ps 27:8).

Fast and pray for your spiritual growth before you pray for other things like buildings or money. I'm more aware of my sins and failures when I fast than at other times in my spiritual walk with God. Since a godly person like Paul said, "Christ Jesus came into the world to save sinners, of whom I am chief" (1 Ti 1:15), I surely can't overlook my sins. I find that the more I fast and the deeper I pray, the more failure God reveals to me. I confess them to God and get His cleansing. It's then that I get on praying ground. When there's no barrier between the Lord and me, then I can ask for great things.

Tie your fast to your life vision. I live a fast-paced life because I have so much to do. Fasting slows me down and gives me time to get the big picture from God. Because my body is not digesting food when I'm fasting, it slows down. Then I go back to evaluate the vision God has given me. Since vision and long-range plans are imperative for any work for God, it's while fasting that we get spiritual vision and spiritual determination. Remember, "Where there is no vision, the people perish" (Pr 29:18, KJV). I include in this verse, churches perish, Christian universities perish, and individual Christians perish. Fasting keeps our spiritual determination sharp.

If you've never fasted, begin with a one-day fast. I teach the people at Thomas Road Baptist Church the Yom Kippur fast, which is from sundown to sundown. Begin by missing the evening meal, and spend time praying that you would have spent in preparing food and eating. Then pray through breakfast and lunch, even though you go about your normal duties. Don't eat until the sun goes down.

Some don't even drink water; this is called an *absolute fast*. However, others drink liquids; this is a *normal fast*. Some fast from certain foods for an extended period of time; this is called a *partial fast*. Daniel ate only vegetables for this kind of fast. Some fast from sports, leisure reading, or television, giving that time to prayer.

Write out your requests for which you're praying, and ask God to give you a prayer promise from the Word of God. If possible, get a partner to fast and pray with you. Your accountability and fellowship with each other will keep you both focused on God's will.

Link the severity of your crisis to the severity of your fast. Many times I've fasted one day as I face the normal problems at the church or university. Sometimes I fast one day just to know God, although there are no pressing problems. But the greater the crisis, the longer you spend in prayer and fasting. Sometimes the greater the problem, the more people you should get to fast and pray with you.

However, a forty-day fast is an extreme activity. I don't recommend this to most reading this book. Most should fast one day. That was the normal expected prayer activity in Scriptures. Before going on a forty-day fast, make sure you absolutely have the leading of God. And finally, don't forget the sequence. Fast first to know God; second, fast for vision; then fast for money or for the crisis in your life.

Experiencing Faith

Identify a request. Look through your list of prayer requests to determine what request is large enough to demand a one-day fast.

But don't fast yet. Write the following along with your other requests: "Should I fast about _____?" Make sure you have the mind of God, even for a one-day fast.

Schedule a day. Make sure you don't have any conflicting events on the day you schedule your fast. For example, don't schedule a fast when you have an important business lunch or a family celebration like a Thanksgiving dinner. Schedule a day in the future where you can give uninterrupted time to prayer and fasting.

Clearly write the reason. Here you should write two things: first, why you are fasting, that is, the prayer request; second, what you want God to do.

Plan your daily schedule. Before you begin the day, block off the mealtimes for prayer. Put it in your planner and treat your prayer time just as importantly as a business meeting.

Gather resources. If I'm praying about hiring a person, I get that person's personnel file and reread it while praying. Many times I've spread bills before God on the bed as I kneel. When I place my hands on the actual bill, my prayers become more urgent. Also, I set aside devotional articles or chapters in a book on spiritual foundations to read while fasting. These are usually longer in length, so I don't have time to read them during a normal busy day.

Pray. Don't get so focused on the mechanics of fasting that you forget to pray. I used to look forward to going on long dates with Macel before we were married. I have the same anticipation when planning to fast. Look forward to spending long hours with God in prayer, fellowship, meditation, and intercession.

Suggested Reading: Ezra 8:21–36; Matthew 6:16–18

DAY 22

Having Continuous Revival

"O Lord, You have searched me and known me."

(Ps 139:1)

Why are our prayers so mechanical or meaningless? Sometimes in church a person will lead in public prayer, but no one is moved. Nothing happens. As impossible as it may seem, prayer can be meaningless and empty.

But there are prayer meetings that change things. Sometimes when people pray, the Spirit of God is felt in the room. Sometimes a person is released from addiction, or a home is put back together, or a church is revived. What's the difference between life-changing prayers and empty prayers?

Today's reading will point out the fertile ground that grows life-transforming prayers. Maybe your prayers are sterile at times. When you pray, your words bounce off the ceiling. You can touch God with your prayers and then, as a result, God will touch you.

When you get through to God to talk to Him, you can transform an otherwise humdrum day into a Spirit-motivated day. Today can change your life because you meet God in a new way.

The Secret of Our Success

One of the greatest prayer warriors I have ever known was a man everyone simply called Brother Worley (Richard Crawford Worley). He was one of the pastors and deacons in the early days at

Thomas Road Baptist Church. If ever I had been sick and needed healing, I would have called for Brother R. C. Worley. The same with a financial problem, or any problem—Brother Worley could get hold of God in prayer. When you have a problem, you want someone like Brother Worley to pray for you.

Why was he so effective? It wasn't the technique he used in prayer, neither was it the way he folded his hands or knelt before God. Whether our prayer is a petition, communion, confession, or worship, it's never a *method* that gets results. Brother Worley was effective in prayer because he lived prayer. He constantly talked with God as he went about his duties. When the two of us visited a home in our community, before we got out of the car, he'd put his hand on my shoulder and say, "Let's pray."

One of the most sanctified places for prayer in our early ministry was an old compressor room in back of the original Donald Duck bottling plant. Brother Worley gathered a group of men for prayer every Sunday evening before the preaching service. I wasn't there, because I was downtown with the local ABC-affiliate, preaching the gospel. So, it was not just my preaching on television that got results, but a group of men who gathered in the most unlikely of all places—the air-compressor room. The presence of God invaded that room and, from it, influenced every area of our church.

In the early days, there was no floor in that room, only dirt. The men dragged in a sheet of plywood and a couple of old used carpets. There were no chairs to sit upon, no benches, and certainly not a fancy prayer altar. The men knelt on the rugs and plywood to pour out their hearts to God. It's not where you pray that gets results. God always looks on the heart, and He honored the deepest yearning of these men. More than anything else, those men wanted God to touch Lynchburg through our church and eventually touch the world.

I can hear Brother Worley say, "We are not worthy of your blessing . . ." Those men came, pouring out their hearts, their souls, their everything. Brother Worley would cry out for God to search him and know him, just as today's verse says, "O Lord, You have searched me and known me" (Ps 139:1). Before you can get on praying ground, you have to see yourself as God sees you. And when you get to that place, it's not a pretty sight.

Brother Worley wanted to know what God saw in his heart. We all have hidden sin in our hearts, hidden pride, hidden doubts, and areas not yielded to Him. Many times we don't realize these things clog the channel of God's mercy. When you have gunk in a fuel line of a car, you have no power because the gasoline can't get through. In the same way, when you have sin in your life you have no power, because sin blocks God's access to you and your access to God.

The good news is that you can know what God knows about you. You can see yourself through God's eyes. David asked, "Search me, O God, and know my heart; try me, and know my anxieties; and see if there is any wicked way in me" (Ps 139:23–24).

Revived by God

When you get honest, the Spirit of God is able to do His work in your heart. He will begin to show you what you are like, and you won't always like what you see. He will show you your sin and transgression; He'll show you where you have fallen short in your service for Him.

The men in that little air-compressor room didn't confess their sins to one another. They all knew one another, and they knew they fell short of God's standards, though they were godly men who did all they could to live according to the standards of the Bible. Brother Worley would lead the way, "Lord, I am unfit; I am a sinner in Your sight. . . ." He didn't name his sin; he simply acknowledged he was a sinner. That's where heaven-opening prayer begins.

There are times when we call our sins by name, like a little boy who wants something from his mother, so he admits what he did to get it. But public confession to get something is not always the path to revival and the work of God in your midst. Don't get me wrong; there is a time to confess specific sins before God. But what I am talking about is an attitude. Our attitude is more important than our words of prayer or our techniques of prayer.

Begin by recognizing you are sinful and unworthy of God's blessing. This is the path to power. When you recognize that you are not worthy to get God's blessings, and you see how far short you fall of God's standards, only then is God able to pour out His power upon you.

In the great New Hebrides Revival, a group of men gathered twice a week for prayer in an old barn among the bales of hay. For three months they prayed, but revival didn't come until one night a young deacon quoted this question from Scripture, "Who may ascend into the hill of the Lord? Or who may stand in His holy place?" (Ps 24:3). He began to hold his hands up, recognizing the awfulness of his sin. Then he answered, "He who has clean hands and a pure heart" (v. 4). He began to cry and asked God, "Are my hands clean?" Revival swept the entire region when one man recognized that he was unfit to stand before God. God had answered his prayer by showing him his sinfulness.

Two steps are necessary to lead you to revival. First, let God show you your sinfulness in light of His holiness. Second, make sure your hands are clean before God. When you have clean hands and a pure heart, then you will be able to pray with power. Then you should get results from your prayers.

What about purity of heart? Purity is a word not heard often in today's society. But I believe Brother Worley and those men in the compressor room—not theologically educated, not ordained in ministry, not men who had risen to the height in the business world, but men who simply believed God—were the ones who moved the hand of God to work through their new church. These men and their wives were faithful prayer warriors; these were the ones who were responsible for the tremendous growth of Thomas Road Baptist Church.

Revival is not a meeting you place on the church's spring calendar, nor is it emotional fervor. Let me define revival. When a person faints and comes back to consciousness, he has been revived. When a backslidden church that has sinned or neglected the work of God comes back to God, that's revival.

In the early days, Thomas Road was in a constant state of revival because of the prayers of these men and women. The Bible defines revival as "I will pour out My Spirit upon all flesh" (Ac 2:17). Again, revival is defined as "times of refreshing . . . from the presence of the Lord" (Ac 3:19). God poured out His Spirit in revival on our new church Sunday by Sunday, as the Holy Spirit was working in the hearts of believers and their friends.

I worked as hard as any young pastor can work—fourteen to sixteen hours a day—but hard work alone never built a church. We constantly waited for the Spirit of God, and when He came, He brought revival to Lynchburg, Virginia. The result was the growth of Thomas Road Baptist Church, Liberty University®, and ultimately the influence of the Moral Majority.

Experiencing Faith

Where does God want to use you? And how is sin (your sin or the sins of others) holding you back from full usefulness? God wants to use you, and He wants to use your church. Here are some steps to greater faith and greater usefulness. *Add a prayer request.* If you have never prayed for revival in your church, add it to your list of requests and begin asking God to pour out His Spirit on your church. Do the same for your personal life; ask for God's revival in your life and service.

Admit you've fallen short. You can get through to God when you admit that you've fallen short and you are not perfect. "If we say that we have no sin, we deceive ourselves, and the truth is not in us" (1 Jo 1:8). When we admit we've fallen short, then our humble attitude properly prepares us to enter God's presence.

Confess your sins. You get forgiveness and cleansing when you confess your sins. "If we confess our sins, He is faithful and just to forgive us our sins and to cleanse us from all unrighteousness"

(1 Jo 1:9). Notice, you don't have to confess to people (unless you've sinned against them); you begin by confessing to God. Maybe you should stop reading and do that now.

Learn from your failures. Every sin is a failure to live the way God requires. So when you confess your sins, you not only tell God you're sorry, but you tell Him you repent. You're turning from that sin. To seal the lesson, you ought to write down what you've learned from your repentance and confession. When you write down these lessons, you're telling God you will live a different life.

Rejoice in God's forgiveness. Once you've dealt with your sin, claim His presence and blessing. Now you're on praying ground. Notice David's testimony after God forgave his sin, "Restore to me the joy of Your salvation, and uphold me by Your generous Spirit" (Ps 51:12).

Suggested Reading: Psalm 139

DAY 23

Thinking the Unthinkable

"Now to Him who is able to do exceedingly abundantly above all that we ask or think, according to the power that works in us."

(Ep 3:20)

I am sure that you want to develop faith that is worthy of our Lord. If you have faith to move mountains, but you've never moved a mountain for God, does that honor Him? No. All of us have different capacities of faith, and we serve God in different ways, but when we exercise our faith, it will show in our outward life.

The whole purpose this month is to develop your faith to believe God for greater things than you've ever done before. So the best way to illustrate a faith-stretching experience is to relate the many things God did for us in the summer of 2004.

When I first began my ministry, I read that God could do "exceedingly abundantly above all that we . . . think" (Ep 3:20). I was a pretty big dreamer, so I didn't think God could do more than I could dream. But God did it.

Don't let the great number of answered prayers in this reading overwhelm your faith. When you start small—as I did, with a Sunday school class of one—and take the next step, you'll keep growing if you keep following the Lord's guidance. Let this chapter challenge you to take the next step of faith in front of you. Then one day you'll see the biggest thing ever happen in your life.

The Biggest Summer Ever

Many Christians have it wrong; they think the blessing of God is measured by the size of buildings, the amount of money in the budgets, or other quantifiable items. But God is not impressed with the amount of money a ministry has or with the size of its buildings. God's emphasis is on people—winning them to Christ, building their faith, delivering them from harmful addictions or false worship, and leading them to be worshippers of Him. I believe God has blessed Thomas Road Baptist Church and Liberty University® because our emphasis has always been on reaching and building up people.

However, in the summer of 2004, everything on Liberty Mountain came together: an abundance of new buildings, paved roads, sports facilities, and much more. It was all for the purpose of reaching and transforming more people in more ways—more than we've ever done before. When someone asked me to explain why we got so many answers to prayer, I said, "[He] is able to do exceedingly abundantly above all that we ask or think, according to the power that works in us" (Ep 3:20).

Originally, God gave us more than four thousand acres on Liberty Mountain, then He gave us the Ericsson manufacturing plant of 888,000 square feet. Those miracles were a prelude to a miraculous summer in 2004. Liberty University® had 2,943 new students, pushing the total enrollment on campus to 8,453 students. That's a tidal wave of young people who want the unique educational experience of Liberty University®. Because God gave us so many students, He had to give us buildings to sleep them, food to feed them, paved lots to park their cars, classrooms to teach them, and gyms and athletic fields for their recreation.

During this time, Liberty completed 19 new dormitories, each one four stories, holding a combined total of roughly 1,600 more students than the university could sleep the previous year. These dorms were located on the east side of the expressway and were connected to the main campus by a walking tunnel that cost the university $1,000,000. Also on the east side of the campus we built a swimming pool, gym, weight room, and cafeteria, all that summer.

Since faith moves mountains, we moved the dirt off an unusable hill to construct a 1,000-space parking lot and filled in an unusable sixty-foot deep ravine next to the football stadium, which became a second 1,000-space parking lot.

Liberty received a $4,500,000 gift for a football operations center, a new two-story building at the north end of the football field with Jeffersonian columns through which people enter. It became the main entrance into the stadium.

Inside the old Ericsson plant we constructed a new student center with five basketball courts and a new NCAA regulation-size pool for sports competition. We built an exercise and weight room with hundreds of exercising machines. Also moving into Ericsson was the new Liberty University® School of Law, the Liberty Baptist Theological Seminary, Bible Institute, and the College of Arts and Sciences. Liberty began building an ice hockey rink and facilities. That year Liberty was ranked number 7 in the NCAA division I colleges.

Now let me tell you about some *big* things. We signed a contract with Kodiak Construction to begin construction of a 6,500-seat sanctuary on the campus for Thomas Road Baptist Church. It will be ready for occupancy in 2006. Also, a seven-million-dollar contract was signed with Kodiak to refurbish the north end of Ericsson into classrooms for Sunday school and the Lynchburg Christian Academy, a 1,200-student day school, pre-kindergarten to high school.

Did I mention we spent almost five million dollars on a new legal library for the new law school? We will train lawyers to uphold the Constitution and defend Christian organizations against the onslaught of secularists and anti-Christian influences. Also, we founded the Jesse Helms School of Government to train students to work in government.

Without a doubt, in 2004 we saw more answers to prayer, moved to have more students educated, and spent more money than ever in a single period of time—more than $55 million—and we didn't have to borrow. God supplied in a magnificent way.

Principles for Receiving Big Things

What big thing is on your list of dreams for your family or your ministry? What is at the top of your prayer list—or would be, if you had the courage to ask for it? We've been looking at the ways God delights to answer, and the things that are close to His heart. So how do you know if your dreams are His dreams?

First, *put your emphasis on people, then trust God to supply buildings, programs, or money.* Too often Christians put their emphasis on raising money for a church auditorium or a youth building. Their whole prayer focus is getting property or things. While these things are necessary, they are never primary. Buildings become obsolete and crumble with time, but your ministry invested in people endures forever.

There have been lots of times that God hasn't answered prayer for property or buildings, or for money to launch out into new ministry ventures, and people wonder what's wrong with their faith. Some have even doubted God or given up the ministry because they didn't get physical things for which they prayed. What's wrong? Maybe their life and ministry suffered because they never learned the priority of people in ministry.

In the second place, you must *excel in the work to which God called you.* Liberty University® attracts an abundance of students because it has outstanding educational programs. Our influence is not measured just by accreditation bodies, such as regional accreditation, nursing accreditation, teacher accreditation, and sports accreditation. Liberty is known by the accomplishments of its graduated students. Some of the great megachurches in America and around the world were planted and pastored by our graduates. Our graduates have gone on to excel in medicine, law, dentistry, education, and sports. They have made it to all the major sports leagues in the United States.

Third, *the blessings of God surround spiritual integrity.* If you emphasize what God emphasizes, you'll get God's blessing. God wants you to emphasize the Bible. It is His Word that changes lives. Every year every faculty member at Liberty must sign agreement to the inspired Word of God. But signing is not enough to get God's attention. We teach Bible classes to every student, because no one is wholly educated until he or she knows the Word of God.

But Liberty takes the Bible one step further—our students and faculty must live daily by the standards of the Word of God. The *Liberty Way*—our student handbook—requires separation from obvious sins such as addictive drugs, premarital sex, etc. But these are not just legalistic standards. Liberty has weekly prayer meetings on each floor of each dorm, there's a spiritual life director on every floor to work with the students, and Liberty requires convocations every week where the Word of God is preached. God blesses Liberty financially because we put Him first and attempt to live godly lives.

In the fourth place, remember that *God responds to simple childlike faith.* Faith is taking God at His Word, no matter what the circumstances dictate. By faith we recruit students, knowing the Liberty experience will transform their life. By faith we teach them the Word of God, knowing the Bible will build character and direct their lives. By faith we send students into all the world to obey the Great Commission, knowing God will use them.

We're not smarter, stronger, or more gifted than others; we just believe what God promised and act on it. When we do what God commands, we can count on God's promise, "My God shall supply all your need according to His riches in glory" (Ph 4:19).

Experiencing Faith

Think big. What's the biggest thing you want God to do for you? That's a good question, but this second question is the important one. If money were not the issue, what is the biggest thing you would do for God? Notice I reversed who does the action. The first question is where most Christians are located; they want God to do something for them. But to develop dream-reaching faith, you must be willing to step out in service to God. If you do, you will see God reward with His blessings.

Check your dream. Make sure the big thing you want from God is something God wants to give you. Sometimes we don't get our dreams because our selfish ambition is in the way. "You ask and do not receive, because you ask amiss, that you may spend it on your pleasures" (Jam 4:3). At other times we dream for big things but are not willing to pay the price of diligent study, hard work, or patient prayers. You must honestly ask yourself these questions:

- Is it biblical?
- Who gets the credit?
- Have I grown enough to receive it?
- Would others glorify God when they see the results?
- Would it harm my continued growth in Christ if I receive it?
- Will lost people come to Christ?
- Will the body of Christ be edified?

Revisit your dreams. Go back in your journal to Day 9 to read again your *life dream*. What would you add/take away from your statement as a result of today's lesson? Write your *life dream* again, looking at it through your expanded understanding of faith. Write what you would do for God if money were not an issue.

Pray your dream. Now that you've upgraded your *life dream*, commit yourself to pray earnestly for its completion. "Faith is the substance of things hoped for, the evidence of things not seen" (He 11:1).

Suggested Reading: Philippians 4:1–20

DAY 24

Sympathy in Action

"And on some have compassion, making a difference."

(Jude 22, KJV)

We've been talking about developing your faith; now let's talk about how to have faith as you minister to others. You won't get great mountain-moving faith just to have it. Growing your faith is like developing strong muscles. You must continually use your muscles or you will lose your strength.

During this month you've been developing your faith, and we've talked a lot about getting your prayers answered. Now it's time to put your faith to work and make a difference in someone's life.

In this lesson we'll talk about breaking bad habits or even dealing with some form of addiction. Think of someone whose addiction breaks one of the Ten Commandments, such as sexual addiction or being a compulsive liar, or one who continually takes God's name in vain. Some people harm themselves with addiction to alcohol or drugs. Others have more mundane habits they'd like to break, such as a compulsive eating habit. Some of these problems are just beginning, and others are a death-grip addiction.

What about you? Is something holding back the development of your faith? Maybe you'd like the water-walking faith of Peter, but you can't even get out of the boat. When you learn the steps in this lesson, you'll have a greater faith than ever. And if you have someone in your life with harmful habits, you'll be better prepared to help connect the person with God.

Faith Directed to Help Others

Because my father was an alcoholic and he died of cirrhosis of the liver, I always wanted to go the extra mile in helping people overcome alcohol dependency. As a young pastor, it seemed that almost every day I was meeting a person, usually a man, who was struggling against the power of alcohol. I was praying with these men, and they were being converted; but most of them went back to the bottle. From the beginning I knew that something more had to be done to help them recover and keep them on the straight and narrow path.

Then one Friday afternoon in the winter of 1958, George Ragland entered my office and told me the story of his struggle against alcoholism. I wanted to act quickly, but I had learned by then that sometimes acting without praying can be a disaster. I shared my burden with the deacons at Thomas Road Baptist Church and eventually with the congregation.

God's Spirit led us as we prayed. I began to feel that we needed a farm somewhere deep in the woods and a long distance from bars, restaurants, and liquor stores, where the men could dry out and find comfort and strength within a Christian community. My brother Lewis owned a 165-acre farm at Stonewall, Virginia, just eighteen miles from Lynchburg, yet isolated from the old haunts and the old drinking buddies that plagued my alcoholic friends, and he agreed to let us use the property.

Earl "Look Up" Thompson and George Ragland were the first men at our experimental farm for alcoholics. I called it Elim Home for Alcoholics after the Old Testament story of Elim in the wilderness, an oasis of cool bubbling waters for Israel as they marched those forty years in the wilderness (Ex 15:27).

Our Elim was cold and isolated, but it was an oasis. There was no electricity, and we heated the old drafty building with fireplaces. The two men began their treatment with hope, the first hope they had felt in years. Our associate minister made them welcome, and he supplied a lot of blankets. He taught them every morning from the Word. They performed household and farm chores. They fished and hunted together in the afternoons. They studied the Scriptures again each evening, then prayed together before bedtime.

I stepped out in faith to begin Elim Home. In my early days I didn't have a lot of mountain-moving faith, but I knew a mountain-moving God. I believed God wanted me to do something, and I knew God would bless those who gave attention to the great needs of people.

I couldn't do much, so I did what I could. The facilities were inadequate and the finances were tight, but the ministry was powerful and God was in it. Little did I know how God would meet our needs and make a difference.

A news reporter, James Murdock from the *Daily Advance,* visited Elim Home in January 1959, writing an honest yet compassionate account of what our church was trying to accomplish in this isolated, rather primitive farmhouse in Stonewall, Virginia. It was the first time any story about the ministries of Thomas Road Baptist Church was transmitted throughout the world over the wires of the Associated Press. The results were staggering.

Suddenly we were flooded with applications to come to Elim Home from alcoholics and their families. In just a few weeks the farmhouse was filled with alcoholics.

Just two days after the article appeared, a helicopter landed in a pasture near the farmhouse. James Cooke, the executive director of an electrical cooperative for several counties of Virginia, followed by his key aides, came to survey that old farmhouse. Mr. Cooke determined to help us.

"The nearest electric line is over one mile up the road," Cooke reported after a quick tour of Elim Home. "But I've called on my radio for a crew, and you'll have power here right away."

"But we don't have any wiring in the house," I answered

sheepishly, "and we don't have any money to hire somebody to wire it."

Again Mr. Cooke had the solution. He had already called the right person for help. "I've called Dan Candler," he said. Dan Candler owned Mid-State Electric Company. "Dan will get your place wired," Mr. Cooke promised, "and will throw in a few other little things as well."

A complete wiring job was followed by truckloads of stoves, refrigerators, heaters, and various appliances. Then came a plumbing supply-house truck and crew to put in bathrooms, and a septic company to dig and install a septic tank.

The rules of Elim were (and are) simple. The men must come voluntarily. They cannot be consigned to Elim Home by wife or court. They must come sober. Elim is not a drying-out place; it is a place for total deliverance. The men must sign themselves in. They must quit drinking "cold turkey," without the aid of other chemicals or continued small doses of alcohol. They can't leave in less than sixty days, and they must participate freely in the activities of the Home.

The men are individually counseled by Christian professionals. They work together in small groups. They pray and study the Scriptures together. They learn vocational skills. They hunt and fish and hike the trails. Thousands of men have been through the program. And for the past forty-six years the Elim Home has consistently had a list of men waiting for treatment, two or three months long.

Steps to Freedom in Christ

We have found there are several steps to approach a person with a terrible addiction. Perhaps you need to follow these steps to help someone, or you need these steps yourself. In fact, these steps are necessary to break any sinful habit, not just the obvious ones such as drug or alcohol addiction, or addiction to pornography.

First, *the person must be a Christian.* God won't help someone break a sinful habit unless the person is a Christian. All men at Elim attend Thomas Road Baptist Church Sunday morning, Sunday evening, and Wednesday prayer meeting. We also have a daily evening chapel at Elim, as well as Bible study at the breakfast table.

Many men come to Elim thinking they are Christians, but after they get in the Word of God, they realize they are not believers. Many are then led to Christ personally; most of the men walk the aisle at church and pray to receive Christ at Thomas Road Baptist Church. The best help a man has to quit alcohol is having Christ in his life. But becoming a Christian hasn't helped all alcoholics. Their sins are forgiven, but the poison is in their system and the habit is in their mind. They have to "dry out" and learn new habits. They have to learn to walk in the Spirit (Ga 5:22).

Second, *a believer needs support.* People need to know someone is with them in their struggles. But more than the *presence* of someone else is needed. They need love and encouragement. They need to hear, "You can do it" and "I'm here to support you." Nothing will help alcoholics more than being with people who love them and want them to remain sober. But life at Elim is more than staying sober; it's walking in the Spirit, letting the Holy Spirit control each man's life.

To break old habits and patterns requires learning new habits and skills in the Christian life. The men at Elim learn how to walk in the Spirit by attending church services, chapel, and Bible study. I think the Bible study around the breakfast table is probably the most important thing we do for them. They ask questions and get answers. They listen to the questions and struggles of others. Elim pastors answer their questions. But the men who've been there for a while begin answering the questions of the new arrivals. When a man helps another, he's helping himself.

Becoming accountable to others is the next step. The men are accountable to their roommate and their counselor at Elim. They are accountable for keeping their room clean, attending meetings on time, and performing some tasks and/or ministry. Some work in the vegetable garden that provides some of the food they eat. Others have helped in ministry tasks. In the early days the church had a full print shop and the men helped with non-technical printing tasks.

The final step is to *expect God to work.* Before coming to Elim, the men lived with the high expectation of family and friends that they quit drinking. Although we want that, we try not to give them more guilt about drinking, because that only compounds their problem. Our expectation is for them to walk in the Spirit, not just to quit drinking. We want Christ to dwell in them and live His life through them. That's a much higher standard than getting sober. When they live for Christ, they experience God's power to get victory over alcohol.

Wait for God's miracle. Sometimes it takes patience and loving help. About 50 percent of the men come back a second and even a third time. Steve Jones, one of my present prayer partners, came back to Elim five times before he got victory over alcohol. Now Steve is one of the regular evening chapel speakers at Elim, giving his testimony of God's deliverance. He has a job as an engineer in a local business.

The greatest promise of help to an alcoholic is found in Scripture, "No temptation has overtaken you except such as is common to man; but God is faithful, who will not allow you to be tempted beyond what you are able, but with the temptation will also make the way of escape, that you may be able to bear it" (1 Co 10:13).

Experiencing Faith

Whether your sins and habits are as difficult as a major addiction or as seemingly insignificant as difficulty getting out of bed in the morning, you undoubtedly have some struggles in your life that are holding you back from fully using your time and your gifts in God's service. And in addition, you may know people who face daunting temptations they cannot seem to overcome. God's power is enough to deal with these issues, large or small.

Honestly face your burdens. Perhaps you are in denial about a drinking habit or other problems. God won't help you until you are ready to repent and step away from the sin, and to turn to God for His help. The prodigal son demanded his family inheritance, repudiated his father, and left home for riotous living. Only when he honestly realized what he had done and where he was did his life begin to turn around. "But when he came to himself, he said, 'How many of my father's hired servants have bread enough and to spare, and I perish with hunger! I will arise and go to my father, and will say to him, "Father, I have sinned against heaven and before you"'" (Lk 15:17–18).

List your burden in your prayer journal. This is the first action to help. You could be burdened about a friend or family member, or this could be a personal burden. But do more than write it down; begin asking God to prepare the person's heart for victory. Then ask God to arrange circumstances to start the person on the road to recovery.

Memorize a promise from God. Prayer is only the first step to overcome a habit. There is power in the Word of God, so memorize one of the great promises that God made to help you become victorious over a problem. "No temptation has overtaken you except such as is common to man; but God is faithful, who will not allow you to be tempted beyond what you are able, but with the temptation will also make the way of escape, that you may be able to bear it" (1 Co 10:13).

Exercise your faith, and thank God for victory. Most people who struggle with a problem ask, "What if I fall again?" That negative thought means the person's reliance is in his ability and not in God's power. God will not let us down; we let ourselves down. So focus on God, thank Him for today's victory, and thank Him for today's desires to be victorious over the problem. "Now thanks be to God who always leads us in triumph in Christ" (2 Co 2:14).

Suggested Reading: Galatians 5:16–25

DAY 25

Learning from Mistakes

"All these, having obtained a good testimony through faith, did not receive the promise."

(He 11:39)

W̶e all make mistakes; none of us is perfect. Some people make great mistakes that permanently cripple them or that even take their lives. Others make small mistakes that no one knows about; those mistakes hardly make a ripple on the pond of life.

Whether you have made little or big mistakes, the issue is what will you do about them? Don't let your mistakes discourage you or make you give up. You may react positively to mistakes, step over them and keep going. You may learn vital lessons from your failures and become stronger. You may even use your failures as the greatest classroom of life. You use the lessons learned from your errors to construct an upward road to success.

I made some terrible financial decisions early in my ministry that almost put Thomas Road Baptist Church and Liberty University® out of business. I was ignorant of big business procedures, but God was gracious and our ministry became stronger because of a crisis in the mid-1970s. But most important, I came out of our financial crisis with stronger faith than ever. I felt *If God can help me through this, He can help me through anything.*

I want to help strengthen your faith through failures you face now or will face in the future. Instead of getting discouraged or even thinking about giving up, you can have stronger faith than you have now. Don't despair! God has a way of victory through your problems. Let's find some answers together.

My Greatest Mistake

In April 1973, the U.S. Securities and Exchange Commission began preparing legal charges against Thomas Road Baptist Church and our associates because it claimed we had sold church bonds illegally. Those months of investigation were the most difficult crisis I faced in all my years of ministry to that point. That episode tried my faith more than anything to that date.

We didn't want our case tried beforehand in the front page of the local newspaper and the 6:00 evening news. In spite of our protests, the Securities and Exchange Commission released its claims that we had used "fraud and deceit" to sell $6.5 million in bonds to 1,632 public investors living in twenty-five states. It claimed that Thomas Road Baptist Church "is insolvent in that its current assets were not sufficient to meet its obligations as those bonds became due and payable."

I was devastated when I first got the legal papers. But almost immediately I was encouraged by my inner conviction that I had not intentionally lied or purposely deceived anyone. Mistakes, yes. Fraud, no.

Worse, the Securities and Exchange Commission attorneys claimed that we had not issued a proper prospectus. You can imagine what a field day the journalists had with those charges against us. And you can imagine how our investors, friends, supporters, church members, and the general public felt the first time they read those headlines charging us with insolvency, fraud, and deceit. We were tried in the headlines and found guilty by the public before we could even state our defense in court.

Some fair-weather friends abandoned us, but many who worked in our ministry stayed with us because they knew we were innocent. The students at Liberty University® stayed with us.

The really scary part was the possibility that the Securities and

Exchange Commission might force our church into bankruptcy, put us in "receivership," and padlock our sanctuary and office doors. All before a fair trial.

Today, I want to help prepare you to face your difficulties, just as God helped me in those dark days. First, I admit that we had made mistakes. Our television ministry grew too quickly. The opportunity to move into television across the nation had come without warning. The possibility of beginning a great Christian university needed immediate financing, and we jumped into the bond program without enough experience, without adequate counsel, and without time to do it right.

I learned much from the Securities and Exchange Commission charges that I might not have learned without them. Although we were not insolvent as they claimed, we were really living on the financial edge. In our enthusiasm during that first bond campaign, we had taken foolish, irresponsible risks. Too often our financial records were kept by volunteers who meant well but didn't have adequate training or supervision. We didn't even employ an outside impartial audit firm in those days. We spent money on projects believing that God would provide before we had money to pay for them. That was not so dangerous when we were a little church of thirty-five adult members or even a church of eight hundred, but when we were handling millions of dollars of other people's money, taking certain kinds of risks was irresponsible behavior, and we were quick to admit it.

Though we did not use deceit to defraud, in our excitement to reach our goals we had included some inaccuracies in the bond prospectus. For example, we wrote that the Lynchburg Christian Academy was accredited, when in fact full accreditation was still pending. And we included among the church's assets a large gift, when in fact the donor had only given us a written promise to make that large gift, but had not yet actually transferred the gift to us. (He did make the gift shortly after that, exactly as he promised.)

Perhaps you have heard the terrible expression "evangelistically speaking." It was a popular term to describe evangelists who claimed they were reaching more people than they had actually reached. I hate the expression, but at the time was guilty of it. Lying, half-truths, and exaggerations should be off limits for everybody in public life, especially for those who follow the One who said, "I am . . . the truth" (Jo 14:6). Our intentions may have been good and the figures close to accurate, but we did not meet the required criteria for a bond issue or for strict honesty.

When I was down emotionally, I feared that we might lose everything. These were times that shook my faith to its core, but I never once thought about quitting or giving in. Sometimes I was "up" and dared the enemy. "If we lose everything today," I once said, "we will begin all over again just up the street tomorrow." Through the darkest days, I knew God was with me.

Our lawyers asked the prosecutors to produce one person who had lost one cent. They couldn't produce anyone, because no one had lost anything.

God gave us the victory for which we prayed. The judge took over the supervision of our finances for a short time. He appointed some local men to actually supervise our finances and report to him. Within a short period of time, we paid off the bonds and the judge released us. We were completely vindicated.

How to Turn Failure to Victory

What is your crisis of faith today? Is it difficulty in paying bills? Is it worry over the uncertainty of your husband's job, or concern that the next medical test will reveal that the cancer is still present? Has a loved one or ministry partner hurt you or turned against you? Have you been waiting seemingly forever for God to open the door for a move or a new opportunity?

What role can faith play in your life when you hit a wall or you get discouraged because the odds seem overwhelming? How can you turn a failure into the greatest victory of your life?

First, *get your eyes on God and not on your problem or the op-*

position. I didn't pray without faith for six million dollars in those dark days to pay off our bonds. I was always absolutely convinced God had called me into His ministry. I was absolutely sure God had raised up Thomas Road Baptist Church and opened a door of evangelism through television. I knew God would answer, but I didn't know how. Faith is knowing God will do something, even when you don't know what He will do.

Second, *talk to God continually.* In those dark days, I prayed longer, harder, and more sincerely than ever before. I claimed Mark 11:24, "Whatever things you ask when you pray, believe that you receive them, and you will have them." I knew God was using *The Old Time Gospel Hour,* and I knew the money would come in. So, I kept asking Him to solve our dilemma. And He did!

Third, *get many people praying for you.* I heard somewhere and I repeat it often, "There is value in the volume of prayer." So I got church members praying constantly. Some met daily for prayer during that ordeal. Their prayers not only touched heaven, they touched me and encouraged me. Their prayers demonstrated that they believed in my leadership and the church's integrity. I claimed Jesus' promise, "If two of you agree on earth concerning anything that they ask, it will be done for them by My Father in heaven" (Ma 18:19). My wife, Macel, and I agreed God would intervene, and He did.

Fourth, *never be afraid to examine what you're doing.* Some tried to tell me it was not proper to evangelize by television. Others thought borrowing money—by church bonds—was wrong. So, I examined my motives and knew I was preaching over TV to get people saved. I believed then—as I do now—that God gave TV to everyone, especially the church, to better communicate the gospel to the masses. I faced the question of borrowing money and concluded that I'd need millions to reach the world. If I limited my ministry to the money that my church had, I'd have never carried the gospel to our nation. Television is expensive, but it's powerful. I knew if I talked to Christians all over America, they'd help by giving money to support a television ministry. So, I came to the conclusion that I had done the right thing. But when believers asked honest questions, I had to consider them honestly rather than assume that my first judgment had been correct.

Before you go any further, examine your motives, your practices, and the project you're doing. Faith is doing what God tells you in the Bible, so examine what you do by Scripture.

The fifth principle is *wait for God's release that comes after you admit your mistakes and failures.* I've often said the worst thing in life is not failure in action, but failing to act.

You can't have faith in God without being honest with yourself. When I admitted my mistakes to the judge, the congregation, and the media, I felt a great release. I felt freedom to go forward in ministry but to go about it in the proper way with the proper people, according to the laws of the land. Out of this ordeal, I gained greater faith that was purer and stronger for bigger miracles ahead.

Examining yourself is not the same as "second-guessing" yourself. The standard by which you examine yourself makes the difference. When you examine yourself by the Word of God, you come away stronger because you know God's standard for what you've done, or you can see your failure and repent. On the other hand, when you examine yourself by your results, you may be setting yourself up for discouragement or for giving up. If you do find a problem in your approach or your motives, confess it to God and to anyone who has been hurt by it, and change what needs to be changed.

Finally, when you've applied these five principles, face your failure confidently. Paul reminds us, "Test all things, hold fast what is good" (1 Th 5:21). May God give you faith to face discouragement.

Experiencing Faith

Write a brief profile. Make a few notes in your journal about how you've faced failure in the past. How have you reacted to mistakes in the past? Be honest, because it's the only way you'll develop obstacle-overcoming faith.

Tell God how you'll react in the future. Maybe your faith is weak because you don't know how to climb over your own mistakes. Maybe the way you've reacted to failure in the past is not the right way. So determine what will be your reaction to both little and big self-made problems. "Lord, when I fail, I will _____."

Get proactive about a new strategy to handle failure. Pray and ask God to help you react by faith to any future failures. But prayer is not enough. Proactively apply your new strategy to the next failure, then plan to share your new strategy with a prayer partner or mentor. Ask the person to make you accountable to your new strategy.

Claim victory. Earlier I taught you to make a *faith statement.* That's something you believe God will give you. When you've done everything suggested today, then claim victory by faith. "For whatever is born of God overcomes the world. And this is the victory that has overcome the world—our faith" (1 Jo 5:4).

Suggested Reading: 2 Corinthians 1:3–11

DAY 26

Winning Again After a Big Loss

> "'Naked I came out of my mother's womb, and naked shall I return there. The Lord gave, and the Lord has taken away; blessed be the name of the Lord.' In all this Job did not sin, nor charge God with wrong."
>
> (Job 1:21–22)

Wouldn't it be a wonderful world if our cars never stalled, every business deal worked, our children never disobeyed us, and we never got sick? But that's not life. We live in a troubled world where people get angry or steal, and things go sour. Even Christians mess up.

Why does God allow troubles to plague us if He loves us?

God's purpose is not to give us a trouble-free world, but for us to praise Him in storms. God's plan is not to save us from tragedy, but for us to become stronger in trials. Just as a father takes away his helping hand so his son will learn to walk, so God sometimes removes His hand for a short period so you'll learn to trust Him in all things. And just as the father allows his son to fall several times before the little guy learns to walk, so our heavenly Father lets us fall to learn lessons we could never acquire without falling.

No father wants his son to fall, but the father knows his son will get up to eventually walk. And after walking comes running, and one day the boy may win the high hurdles. Are you learning from the troubles in your life, and learning all that God wants you to know?

If the little boy gave up when he fell, would he ever learn to walk or run? If you give up because of reversals, can you learn what God wants to teach you?

You'll see me smiling on TV or in the pulpit. But I've had plenty of reversals and problems. I don't spend my life complaining about failures or letting disappointments get me down, but I know there are more bad days than good ones for all of us.

Today, let's look beyond our troubles to see what God wants us to do.

Many Long, Dark Nights

I've had several dark nights when I wondered if I would make it to the next day. I've told you about how concerned I was when the Securities and Exchange Commission sued us over fraud. I've told you about almost losing Liberty University® when the Southern Association of Colleges and Schools (SACS) was about to take away our accreditation. There have been physical threats on my life by individuals and a couple of times by mobs in Wisconsin, San Francisco, and Sydney, Australia. The time when finances were so tight I couldn't pay my faculty was a low watermark. Through all of these, it was my God who kept me going.

Suffering by Faith

No one ever suffered as much as a man named Job whose story is described in the Bible. He suffered much more than I ever have. He lost all of his children, his wealth, and his health in a matter of days. There is much we can learn from him about victory in life after we've suffered some of our most difficult hours. His story is one of the most incredible accounts in Scripture, and it reveals the cosmic spiritual struggle that goes on in heaven behind the scenes of this life.

Job, who is introduced in a Bible book that bears his name, was a man of great wealth and substance. He had seven sons and three daughters, and he was blessed with seven thousand sheep, three thousand camels, five hundred yoke of oxen, and five hundred donkeys. By today's standards, Job would have been a Rockefeller or a Bill Gates. He would have driven a Rolls Royce and lived in a mansion. He was wealthy beyond comprehension.

The Scripture also tells us that he was a righteous man who loved God, goodness, and his family. The King James text says that he "eschewed" evil (Job 1:1), meaning that he despised it with all his heart. The Bible also emphasizes that Job's wealth was a blessing from God. Job used his wealth to bring glory to God.

Satan appeared before God to complain that Job served Him only because God had so abundantly blessed him. Satan then challenged God to move against Job and predicted that if God did, Job would turn against Him.

God told Satan, "Behold, all that he has is in your power; only do not lay a hand on his person" (Job 1:12). This text emphasizes a great spiritual truth: Satan has no power over our lives except by the permission of God. So Satan took away all of Job's possessions. Wealth could easily be lost in the ancient East, and bandits stole all his sheep and cattle in one day. His herds were devastated and his servants murdered. Then, before the day was over, all of his children were killed by a desert storm when the house they were in collapsed.

Devastated by these personal tragedies, Job simply responded, "Naked I came from my mother's womb, and naked shall I return there. The Lord gave, and the Lord has taken away; blessed be the name of the Lord" (Job 1:21). The Scripture further explains that in all that happened, Job did not sin against God (v. 22).

Again, Satan came before God, but this time arguing that if he could touch Job's body with illness, Job would turn against God. Satan said, "Stretch out Your hand now, and touch his bone and his flesh, and he will surely curse You to Your face!" (Job 2:4–5).

God refused to let Satan kill His servant Job: "Behold, he is in your hand, but spare his life" (Job 2:6). Satan struck Job with a terrible disease. Job came down with boils that covered his entire body. He had not only lost what he loved most—his children—but now he lost his health as well.

In the next scene, Job is seen sitting in a pile of ashes, pathetically scraping himself with a broken piece of pottery. He had been reduced to the trash pile of life. Can you imagine his suffering and pain? Broken and rejected, he sat there all alone.

Job's friends came to console him, but eventually they ended up accusing him of hiding some secret sin. Their consolation turned to condemnation and criticism. Just when Job thought things could not possibly get worse, they did . . . his wife gave up on him.

His wife cried out in frustration for Job to curse God and die. She would have said in our terminology, "Why fight it? It's not worth it!"

But in all this, Job did not let his faith in God waver. In spite of his personal pain, he learned to keep on living by the grace of God. And because of that faith, God eventually vindicated him and blessed him with ten more children and twice as many possessions as he had originally. Job knew that he could depend on God no matter what went wrong.

We too can learn how to handle life's toughest problems as we come to the realization that when all goes wrong, God's way is right. He is still moving on our behalf wanting our greatest good to come together for His glory. We must trust God in the darkness.

The real question for each of us to ask ourselves is, "How am I doing with my problems?" Has Satan ever bombarded you and gotten you down? Has he ever pulled the rug out from under your life and left you in a heap of ashes? If that is where he has you now, this is no time to quit. When you do get down, you probably get lonely and start to wallow in self-pity. You feel like no one understands your pains and your problems. Remember, it is often darkest before the dawn.

Whenever you're down, you may tend to think that you are the only one suffering in the entire world. You feel like nobody understands or cares. That's when Satan comes along to say, "No one really loves you. You've blown it! Why don't you just give up?"

Whenever the devil tries to beat you down, remember Job. In spite of all his troubles, and even the rejection of his wife and friends, Job hung onto his faith. He put his confidence in God's personal integrity and trusted Him with his very existence. God is always there for us, even when we cannot see Him.

Job's greatest source of strength was the promises of God. He knew in the depth of his heart that he could trust God to be true to His promises. Job knew God could bring him through his troubles. Absolutely nothing can occur in our lives that God has not promised to see us through. So, hang on to God who promises, "I will never leave you, nor forsake you" (He 13:5).

Experiencing Faith

Look in the rearview mirror. You can't live in the past, so why should you let past failures control your future? But sometimes you need a rearview mirror to get a total view of the journey ahead. So today list in your journal two or three past problems that could have destroyed you, but didn't. You might add a few comments why these troubles were threatening. Also, write a brief explanation of how God solved them or helped you live through tough times.

Take your spiritual temperature. Look at your life today to determine what you've learned from past problems. How are you stronger? What did God teach you through your troubles? Maybe God wants to use your present troubles to make you a better person.

Look beyond your present troubles. Since God has used past troubles to make you a better person, don't you think He can do the same thing again? God may have more than one lesson to teach you. Write them in your journal. Identifying what you expect to learn may give you present hope in the dark night. It may help get you through the difficulties.

Consider it a faith issue. What is our usual reaction to troubles? We ask, "Why is this happening to me?" or, "Why is this happening now?" When your whole focus is on your difficulties, you lose God's perspective. When your focus is on God, He shows up as magnificently larger than any troubles you may face.

Make all your difficulties a faith issue. Since God brings troubles to make you stronger and better, when you refuse to learn from your difficulties, you turn your back on God. Accept your difficulties by faith, learn what God wants you to know, and work through today's difficulties by following His principles. "And all these, having obtained a good testimony through faith, did not receive the promise, God having provided something better for us, that they should not be made perfect apart from us" (He 11:39–40).

Suggested Reading: Job 1–2

DAY 27

Rejoicing in Victory

> "So the wall was finished . . . in fifty-two days. And [our enemies and the surrounding nations] perceived that this work was done by our God."
>
> (Ne 6:15–16)

God wants you to be a positive person who rejoices in His work in your life. Each day we've been looking at the different ways God works in your life. We've emphasized how God talks to you, how He prepares you, and how He teaches you lessons through problems. Today, let's look at the victories in your life—big ones and small—so you can learn to be grateful to God. And through praises and gratitude, you can strengthen your faith so that you are ready for God's blessings.

An old hymn tells us to "count your blessings, name them one by one." That does more than make us happy or positive. By systematically thanking God for past victories, we lay a foundation for more future blessings from Him.

No matter what trouble you're now facing, you can change your outlook on life if you'll change inwardly; you can positively influence your circumstances. You can't control the things that happen to you, but you can control the things that happen in you.

Today's reading should make you more positive because you'll review the past victories God has given you. No matter who you are, God has done some good things for you. So today you'll reflect on these things and become stronger in your faith walk with God.

Rejoicing in Victory

Our early efforts to build Thomas Road Baptist Church were like Nehemiah constructing the wall around Jerusalem. He had to reach new people and build new facilities at the same time. We couldn't continue reaching people without additional buildings. And we couldn't pay for the new buildings without new people and the money they would give.

Very early we purchased that little Donald Duck bottling plant and the land on which it stood. Some outsiders laughed and called us the Donald Duck Baptist Church, but we were church owners and we were proud of that little building. Our payments stretched us to the limits. We had the payments on the land and buildings. With $49 a week for radio and $90 a week for television, $17 a week for mimeographing and mailing the newsletter, and my $65 a week salary, we had nothing left to make repairs on the storefront building or to construct additional space needed because of growing crowds. A contractor estimated that we would need almost $5,000 to build the first 30' × 50' addition.

We needed space immediately, so a tent was supplied. I'm not sure where it came from, but it had holes. So we prayed that summer and not one Sunday did we have rain. The tent gave us protection from the sun, and in the fall it brought protection from the cold weather.

"We'll have to borrow the money," I told the men after an evening of discussion with our trustees.

"But with what collateral?" a deacon asked, shaking his head. "Without collateral nobody will lend us that kind of money."

So the next day I visited S. Frank Pratt, the owner of the Lynchburg Oil Company, to ask him how I could secure a loan.

"I'm starting a church, Mr. Pratt," I told him.

"I've heard, Jerry," Frank Pratt answered. "In the old Donald Duck building, isn't it?"

"Yes," I said, not really surprised that he had heard about us with all the noise we had been making. "But we've already run out of space. And the supplies we need to build cost five thousand dollars." Frank Pratt began to smile as he listened.

"We don't have the money, Mr. Pratt," I said, "and our offerings are only a few hundred dollars a week. But with the growth we're expecting, I believe we could pay it all back in just a year or two."

Before I could ask my question, Mr. Pratt picked up the phone and called his man Billy McLeod, who ran State Industrial Loan for him.

"Billy," he shouted over the phone line, "I'm sending Jerry Falwell down there. Let him have five thousand dollars for his church."

Looking back, I remember worrying how we could get the loan without collateral. I should have had more faith. But that five-thousand-dollar loan was the biggest financial victory I'd had up until that time. Even though we hadn't laid a single brick, I rejoiced in God's provision.

One day after getting that loan, our contractor and his crew of volunteers purchased and unloaded on our lot almost five thousand dollars worth of supplies we couldn't afford. Immediately we began to build. We walled and roofed our new thirty-by-fifty-foot addition before adding the floor. We installed little space heaters with exhaust pipes going out the holes where the windows would eventually be. We covered the rest of the window spaces with metal panes to keep out the coming cold. We needed to use the building space before rooms could be finished. We raced against winter weather and met on dirt floors in cold rooms to sing and pray and teach our children.

Our volunteers worked on Saturdays and almost every night of the week until 10 P.M. Men built. Women brought food and drink. Children swept, retrieved, and straightened nails (to save money) or played with pieces of wood and pipe nearby. Just as the neighbors began to complain about the loud sound of hammers and saws that was echoing out across the neighborhood, we completed the first new addition. And the "holey" tent was removed forever.

We had a group of men who believed God wanted us to build a church. They put feet to their faith by sacrificing their time, talent, and treasure for bigger things. I learned faith from them. I couldn't slow down because they were counting on me; I didn't want to slow down because of what God was doing in my heart. My faith, added to their faith. Faith built Thomas Road Baptist Church.

From that day we never stopped building. First we added to the rear of the storefront, adding an additional fifty feet, making it one hundred feet. Then we added thirty-eight feet to the front of the building toward Thomas Road. Our church looked like an extremely long bowling alley, 138 feet long and just 30 feet wide. All this happened in the first year, and immediately every new inch of space was filled by new children and adults coming to the church because our faithful soul winners were witnessing throughout our community.

Steps to Victory

God uses many different gifts in His body, and He gives us many different callings. Perhaps your greatest challenge at this point in your life is getting your baby to sleep through the night and finding a few uninterrupted minutes during the day to read Scripture and go through this book. Or you may be pondering God's calling to a new and scary ministry challenge. Perhaps you are finding yourself prostrate before God pleading for the salvation of a wayward child or an unfaithful spouse. God knows your struggles and heartaches; they don't take Him by surprise or challenge His sovereignty. He is big enough to handle your challenges and the problems of those you love.

The following principles should guide your ministry whether

you're building your family or preaching the Word of God. The principles of constructing a building are similar to the guidelines of building up people. First, *focus on God's presence.* God visited His people in the Old Testament as they worshipped Him under the open sky. There were no tents or buildings for the worship of Adam, Noah, Abraham, Isaac, and Jacob. Only during the forty years in the wilderness was God worshipped in a tent. Then for many generations people worshipped in the tabernacle until Solomon constructed the temple. Even then, the beauty of the temple was not its grandeur; no, its beauty was God Himself. "The [Shekinah glory] cloud filled the house of the Lord, so that the priests could not continue ministering because of the cloud; for the glory of the Lord filled the house of the Lord" (1 Ki 8:10–11).

To me that old Donald Duck red brick building was the most beautiful church in town. I loved that place, even when I had my trousers rolled up to my knees, mopping out sticky syrup from the floors. Its greatness was the presence of God that people felt when they entered to sing to God. Its beauty was the Lord who walked among the rows to convict people of sin and call them to salvation.

Second, *keep your focus on people.* God is not primarily interested in buildings, but on the people in a building. The church is not the building in which Christians meet, even though we call the building a church. A church is people. A home is not primarily a house; it's the people in that house and the way they love one another and serve others. God loves people; He sent His Son to die for people, and now Jesus indwells the heart of His people. The building is just a location where Christians gather for singing, preaching, teaching, and fellowship. What goes on in the building is many times more important than the building itself.

To me, Thomas Road Baptist Church was the greatest church in the world. We had come through a battle to get the church started, and every time we went out to witness the gospel to unsaved neighbors, we were in a battle for their souls. Every time we encountered someone with the gospel, it was part of a larger battle that was going on in Lynchburg. I loved my people, and I loved the challenge of the ministry, and I'll always love the old Donald Duck bottling plant where our church was born; but I love those first members of the church in a much greater way.

The quality of your outward circumstances should reflect the inward ministry of God. When people look at your life, they should see the contentment and love of God radiating from your life. At first we didn't have much, but we did the best we could with what we had. People laughed when they called us the Donald Duck Baptist Church, and someone said the "holey tent" wasn't very holy. There wasn't any comparison between our "makeshift" facilities and the high-steeple churches of the city. We couldn't compete with their organs, hardwood floors, and stained-glass windows. All we had was the power of God to change lives, and that's what people wanted. They flocked to our services because they looked beyond our facilities. They knew Christ was in our church and they could find Him there.

But we didn't keep the old things. We eventually got rid of the old theater chairs, and we didn't stay in the tent. Our third auditorium had stained-glass windows, hardwood floors, and an organ. Our fourth auditorium was distinctively Colonial Jeffersonian. Yet the secret of filling a new, more elegant building with people was the power of the old-fashioned gospel message that I heard from my mother's radio on Sunday mornings. The message remained the same, even though the buildings were modern and streamlined.

Remember, victory is not a destination; it's the next step in your walk of faith. If you always live for victory way out in the future, you won't enjoy a victory God gives you today. The same thing is true if you live in the victories of the past. Today counts! So serve the Lord today, and ask God to help you overcome your obstacles today. Focus on victory today.

Life is a walk of faith where we continually confront and overcome obstacles. When the Bible tells us to live "from faith to faith" (Ro 1:17), it also means we go from victory to victory.

Experiencing Faith

Today, let's strengthen your faith by reviewing your victories. Let's learn from the past how to face today's obstacles and get victory.

List praises. Make a list of the ten things for which you are most thankful. This is a good exercise that encourages your faith to keep going on for God. Write the list in your journal. Some of these things are victories; other things on your list might be wonderful things God has brought into your life. Whatever the reason that God has given them to you, they should make you a grateful person.

Put an asterisk next to obvious victories. Mark your victories and make some notes in your journal about what these victories mean to your growth and faith. Gratitude grows your character.

Purposefully praise God for your victories and what they mean to you. You will grow your faith as you tell God how grateful you are for His victories in your life. Praise makes you look at your life through the eyes of God, and when you have a God-oriented life, you'll gain strength to overcome future obstacles and win future victories.

Suggested Reading: Acts 18:1–11; Nehemiah 4; 6:15–16

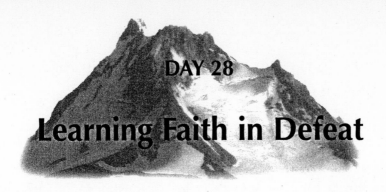

Learning Faith in Defeat

> "... knowing that the testing of your faith produces patience."
>
> (Jam 1:3)

Y ou will overcome some problems in this life quickly, completely, and triumphantly. But some obstacles may eat at you
like slowly rotting timbers for the rest of your life. Some problems
will crash into you head-on and hurt you, or even permanently
maim you. Some problems you may never defeat. That's not nec-
essarily lack of faith; the apostle Paul had such an experience by
God's choice (2 Co 12:7–10). But many of God's people can tell stories of seemingly insurmountable struggles that God has removed.
So keep praying until God answers or gives a clear no.

In this chapter, let's talk about striving against obstacles when
you can't see victory on the horizon. Let's discuss those obstacles
that seem formidable and that it appears you'll never win over in
this life. How can you keep your faith strong when fighting an op-
ponent that you can't seem to defeat? What happens to your faith
when you are defeated?

Undoubtedly you've suffered reversals and you've experienced
losses. But remember, faith is not based on any victory you've ever
won. Your faith is based on the Word of God. You must do what
God wants you to do, whether or not you are successful.

Take courage if you're struggling against a problem that seems to
have no answer. If you've been struggling a long time, this lesson

will give you hope in your difficulties and how to strengthen your faith. This may be the most important reading thus far.

A Difficult Battle

On January 23, 1973, a story in our *Lynchburg News* radically affected my life and the life of my family. "Yesterday, in the landmark *Roe v. Wade* decision, the Supreme Court ruled unconstitutional all state laws that prohibit voluntary abortions before the third month. Feminists hail the decision as an important breakthrough for their cause. Right-to-life opponents of the decision promise to fight for a constitutional amendment banning abortions."

The Supreme Court made a decision by a seven-to-two margin that legalized the killing of millions of unborn children. I could not believe that seven justices on the nation's highest court could have so little regard for the value of human life.

I don't usually let the newspaper interfere with my breakfast with the family, but on that day my coffee grew cold and my family ate alone. I sat there staring at the *Roe v. Wade* story, growing more and more fearful of the consequences of the Supreme Court's act and wondering why so few voices had been raised against it. Hoping that words would be enough, I began to preach regularly against abortion, calling it "America's national sin." However, it soon became apparent that preaching would not be enough.

Opponents to the *Roe v. Wade* decision were protesting in the streets. But such a step was entirely against my nature. So I began to reread relevant biblical passages to find out what to do. I prayed long and earnestly for God's Spirit to enlighten me. I talked about this life-and-death issue to my friends and even to my enemies. And I tried to stay open to the truth, even when it seemed to threaten my past convictions.

Also, I became concerned that taking a political stand, even on my own time, might divide our growing congregation. I pastored a pluralistic church where people could hold various political views and still be one in Christ. Already the nation was being terribly divided over the issue of abortion. Would that also happen to my congregation?

One evening during devotions with my family, I confessed my own growing need to do more than preach against the Court's decision. I shared my fears about the death of generations of unborn children. My family sat in a little circle around the fireplace and listened. I was afraid that our children might be too young to understand the details of such a painful issue. But I knew that whatever decision I made would affect their lives as well as mine. Macel agreed that it seemed irresponsible for me to exclude them from the decision-making process.

Jonathan was only 7, but his eyes filled with tears as I described the meaning of abortion and its effects on the unborn and their mothers. Jeannie was 9. She grew noticeably angry when she heard about the suffering.

That night, right or wrong, I confessed my fears to my family. I doubted seriously that America could survive the judgment of God because of this "national sin." Finally I made this statement: "Kids, it is doubtful that you will be living in a free America when you are the same age as your parents."

Jonathan had grown more and more restless as I spoke. When I finished, he got up off the floor, walked over to the fireplace, knelt before me, and placed his hands on my knees. For one moment he looked directly into my eyes without speaking. Then 7-year-old Jonathan asked one simple question that helped change our lives forever. "Daddy," he said, his lip quivering, "why don't you do something about it?"

Jeannie smiled at her little brother in agreement, then looked directly at me. Macel and Jerry Jr. were looking on. They, too, were silent but seemed totally in agreement with Jonathan's words. Finally Macel hugged Jerry Jr., smiled at me with knowing eyes, and stood to end our time together.

"It's time for bed," she said, and the children hugged me one by one and followed Macel toward their bedrooms. Before tucking them in, I sat for a moment by the fire and thought of the words of

Jesus: A little child shall lead them. In that brief moving moment of consensus, our family began a brand-new journey together. Jonathan was absolutely right. I had to do something, and I had to do it quickly.

I think I have done everything spiritually, politically, and physically I could do to reverse the tide of abortion in America. It's one of the biggest fights I've ever picked in my life. We win a few battles against abortion, then we lose some other battle. But it's not over and I'm not giving up.

Gaining Perspective

Let me give you some principles to keep your faith strong when you're not making progress in your fight against an enemy.

First, *you are winning an inner battle just because you've entered the fray.* Some might laugh, thinking I'm just "pumping up" the troops, but I think it was a victory just that we've gotten into the battle against abortion. Think how far the enemy would carry the issue if we had not raised the national awareness against abortion.

And we're winning because of all the young women we have helped and the babies we have saved. Many who would have been killed as babies are alive, walking shopping malls, and, in many cases, spreading the gospel. Maybe we haven't saved as many as the abortionists have killed, but every success brings a smile to God's people everywhere.

Also, we're winning because we've called our faith to battle. If we had given up and not gotten involved, we would have weakened our resolve against evil. We would have defeated ourselves by remaining quiet.

Second, *keep fighting when you're right, not just when you're successful.* If Christians were successful in everything they attempt, the world would follow Christ for the wrong reasons. The world would be saved to be successful. But look at things through faith. You believe in Jesus Christ because He's the truth, not pragmatically because He makes your life better. You believed in Jesus because you wanted forgiveness of sins, and when you chose to follow Jesus, some people probably turned against you. Life didn't get easier, it got more difficult.

Obviously we fight abortion to win, and obviously we fight abortion to put a stop to the killing. But we're in a battle to the end. Abortion is a killing money-machine that will fight us to the death. A permissive sex-crazed society that demands free sex at any time with anyone will not tolerate the elimination of their fire escape. If we could stop abortion, people's "sexual needs" would be compromised. Then there's the biased feminist, who is blinded to the murder she performs so she can have the freedom of her body. Finally, there are liberal judges who protect a liberal way of life. None of our opponents will give up easily. With all these against us, it's hard to make any progress against abortion.

So my faith keeps me fighting, whether we seem to be winning or not. I keep fighting because it's the right thing to do.

Third, *know that we may not win on this earth,* because our victory lap is in heaven. Christians have lost battles before. Outstanding believers have been martyred. Churches have been attacked and worshippers have been burned to death inside. We may not win on this earth, but the battle is not over till after we die. I fight abortion because it's wrong, and God wants me to stand for right and life. I fight abortion because it's the right thing to do, and if I don't win in this life, there is a greater victory in heaven.

Keep your eyes on Jesus. Don't look at the battle, you'll get discouraged. Don't just look for victory; you'll be looking for the wrong thing. We must serve the Lord, and He is our reward.

Faith always takes the long look beyond the grave. So keep fighting your personal battles; keep struggling when you think victory is elusive. Keep your faith strong. "Therefore we also, since we are surrounded by so great a cloud of witnesses, let us lay aside every weight, and the sin which so easily ensnares us, and let us run with endurance the race that is set before us, looking unto Jesus" (He 12:1–2).

Experiencing Faith

When you can't go forward, it's a good time to do an assessment or take an inventory. Ask yourself the following questions. When you come up with the correct answers, your faith ought to be strengthened, even when outwardly you're being defeated. If your answers aren't correct, then make some in-course corrections and get on the right track.

Priority: Is the battle yours or God's? When Goliath challenged the army of Israel to a battle, no one would fight him. Then David asked a question, "Is there not a cause?" (1 Sa 17:29). David determined the battle was not his, but God's. "I come to you in the name of the Lord of hosts . . . whom you have defied" (v. 45). When David knew his motives were right and the battle was justified, he said, "The battle is the Lord's, and He will give you into our hands" (v. 47).

Timing: Should the battle be fought now? Sometimes a battle is worth fighting, but you should wait until you get help or it's the appropriate time to fight. Perhaps tomorrow you'll win the battle that you might lose today. A baby can't win a battle when he's small, but when he is grown to maturity, he can win.

Ultimate goal: Does the struggle fit within your life purpose? We all have a purpose in life. Don't get side-tracked fighting battles that will distract you from the purpose God has for you. God may give this battle to someone else.

Direction: Does the battle help you accomplish your life plan? Remember, you determined a *life purpose,* then you made a strategic plan of sequential cause and effect events that will accomplish your *life plan.*

The battle is God's, and He is able to place His soldiers in the most strategic spots. Find your position, and trust Him for the victory, whether you see it or not.

Suggested Reading: James 1:1–18

DAY 29

Praying with Others

"Again I say to you that if two of you agree on earth concerning anything that they ask, it will be done for them by My Father in heaven."

(Ma 18:19)

Praying with others is one of the great ways to develop life-changing faith. Jesus said if two agreed together, they would get their prayer answered.

I want you to live at a higher level than ever before. I want God to do wonderful things in your life. But you can't accomplish great things for God alone. You plus others is always better than you alone. So in this lesson I want you to find help to grow your faith and reach your potential for God.

Without prayer partners, I'm convinced there wouldn't be a Liberty University®, nor would Thomas Road Baptist Church have the great influence it has. What God has done for me, He has done with the help of many others.

When you agree in prayer with another, you begin to share the other person's heart and the other person's faith. Actually, praying with another to remove mountain obstacles means you exercise your own faith. And isn't exercising the way to strengthen your physical body? Likewise, praying with another will strengthen your faith.

Also, you can receive strength when you agree in prayer with

197

your prayer partner. He or she can give you courage or boldness to pray confidently. And when the other person prays with faith, that will strengthen your faith. And isn't that what you want, stronger faith to fulfill your *life purpose?*

The Prayer of Others

When eternal decisions were being made about Liberty University®, a woman was on her knees praying for me. I had a dream of beginning a unique college that would change the world. I kept looking for a person to help me start a college; I was not an educator. I wanted a unique man who could walk in the world of academics, yet he had to have a heart for God and the local church. More than that, I wanted him to have a great heart for evangelism.

Elmer Towns was a professor at Trinity Evangelical Divinity School in Greater Chicago who wrote the best-seller, *The Ten Largest Sunday Schools and What Makes Them Grow.* Elmer Towns had discovered Thomas Road Baptist Church had the ninth largest Sunday school in America in 1969, and he had interviewed me. He wrote this award-winning book that credited our church growth to great Sunday school evangelism. I found out he had been a Bible college president in Canada and was on a commission for the Accrediting Association of Bible Colleges. I was already thinking he was my man, then I heard from my pastor friends that his sermons had sparked evangelistic outreach at their church.

On the last Saturday evening of January 1971 about 7:00 P.M., I phoned his home in Greater Chicago. His wife, Ruth, told me he was preaching at Canton (Ohio) Baptist Temple, one of the biggest churches in America. Then I said to Ruth, "I've never talked to a man's wife about a job, but would Elmer be interested in starting a college for me?" I could tell from her voice she was excited. Elmer was staying in a bedroom in the church (we call it a prophet's chamber) that didn't have a telephone. So I told Ruth to have Elmer phone me when he called home. She immediately knelt to begin praying for the college, praying for us as we planned it; but most of all she prayed for Elmer to call her.

At 7:00 P.M. when I was talking to Ruth, Elmer was visiting Pastor Harold Henniger, who had had open-heart surgery. I don't think our two conversations at the same time in different cities was a coincidence; *God is in the details of our life.*

Pastor Henniger told Elmer to come help me begin a college. The pastor then told Elmer, "You and Jerry are two peas in a pod. You'll work well together and build a great Christian college."

Elmer told Harold I was years away from starting a Christian college because I was still building an elementary school and a high school. Then Harold made Elmer promise to go back to the church—use a church phone—and immediately call me. As Elmer left Henniger's home, the pastor reiterated his urgency, "Promise me you'll phone him immediately."

Shortly after I hung up with Ruth, the phone rang. It was Elmer Towns. I thought Elmer had phoned his wife first, but he hadn't phoned home. The first thing I asked was, "What should be the college's name?" That was before I even found out if he was interested.

Towns said, "We must determine the purpose of the college before we can determine its name." He said, "I don't think you want to start just a Bible college for full-time workers. You want a college to prepare lawyers, doctors, educators—you want to educate all Christian young people to help capture the world for Christ."

"Amen," I said in my heart.

Just as the oak tree is in the acorn, the greatness of what Liberty was to become was planned in our first conversation.

We determined three things that night. First, we would build a college on *academic excellence*, recruiting the best teachers and students.

Next, we determined to construct an *action-oriented curriculum.* Our college students would be activists for Jesus Christ, teaching Sunday school, counseling in camps, actively involved in "I Love

America" campaigns. They would work in jobs for which they were training as they were educated.

Finally, we decided our education would be on the cutting edge of the future, *yet anchored to the Rock.* We wanted sharp-looking young people, not dressed like they lived in the Middle Ages. In the early days women's dresses were to the knees, no facial hair on men, and all men wore ties. Today, our youth are still modestly dressed, yet culturally relevant, as a testimony to Jesus Christ.

Towns and I talked about several names for the college that evening. Finally we called the new college Lynchburg Baptist College. Later, when our mail got mixed up with Lynchburg College, we changed the name to *Liberty,* a name I love and the name I originally had in my heart for the school.

When Elmer Towns phoned his wife to tell her they would be moving to Lynchburg, she was way ahead of him. She had been praying for an hour, and I believe God heard her prayers. The foundational concepts of Liberty were decided that night when Ruth Towns was praying.

I had many great prayer warriors interceding for my ministry and me. I've already introduced you to my mother. My mom never stopped praying for me, even when I was far from God. When years passed with no signs that her prayers were being heard, let alone answered, she continued to pray for me. She was never melodramatic about it. I never saw her kneeling at her bedside, nor did I ever hear her crying out to God on my behalf. Quietly, patiently, secretly, she prayed for me at the beginning of each day and at its end. And no matter what I did or said, she kept praying. She was also foundational in praying for the establishment of the church and college.

There have been many effective prayer warriors in Thomas Road Baptist Church, including Amanda Horsley, R. C. Worley, Katie Bowles, Pop Johnson, Nancy Godsey, and my secretary, Jeanette Hogan.

But my greatest prayer support comes from my wife, Macel. Many times we've knelt to pray for needed money for projects at the church. I remember when one thousand dollars stretched our faith. But God was faithful to answer these first requests. Then we stretched for a million dollars, and next ten million. Every step of faith I've taken, Macel has been with me.

Finding Prayer Partners

You will want some people to pray for you and with you. *You get prayer partners by asking for them.* Obviously, you ask God to raise up prayer supporters, then He may give you prayer help from the most unlikely places. Ruth Towns interceded for Liberty and me long before I met her. But after you've asked God for a prayer partner, then you must ask people to pray for you. Notice how Paul expressed it, "Brethren, pray for us" (1 Th 5:25).

You must pray for them as they pray for you. A biblical prayer relationship is not just a one-way avenue where a person prays for you. Partnership is of necessity a two-way street. Thomas Road doesn't have just one Wednesday night prayer meeting. We have groups praying together before each church meeting and at various times throughout the week. People wonder how I get so many prayer warriors at Thomas Road and why so many of them are committed to praying for me. It's because I begin every morning praying for them. Paul told the brethren, "I thank my God upon every remembrance of you, always in every prayer of mine making request for you all with joy" (Ph 1:4).

Remember, people can't pray for you if they don't know what you're doing. So you need to *share your requests, dreams, and problems with prayer partners.* But look at that principle again. They won't continue praying for you if you're not aggressively doing something for God. In my ministry, I've kept busy; so I keep my prayer partners busy praying for the next project. And I've always tried to do impossible things, so I keep stretching my prayer partners' faith to ask God for the impossible. "For with God nothing will be impossible" (Lk 1:37).

Sometimes we tend to get independent and self-sustaining. We may think we don't need prayer, or we think our prayers are enough. When we get to that place, we're on dangerous ground. *You need prayer partners even when you don't know that you need them.* God has given me prayer partners who interceded for me over the years, often just when I was making the most crucial decisions about Liberty. I needed them because if I made wrong decisions, I couldn't go back and redo them. So now I publicly thank all my prayer partners. We couldn't have built Liberty if we had not done it together (1 Co 3:9).

Experiencing Faith

Brainstorm. Make a list of people you've successfully prayed with in the past. Write a sentence to suggest why the two of you were successful at prayer. Reviewing your past action will stretch your thinking to help find a prayer partner for the future.

Memorize Matthew 18:19 so you can use it to help find a prayer partner, or use it as a prayer promise when praying.

List potential prayer partners. You should have at least one prayer partner, but you might want more than one. You might pray about family matters with one person—your spouse—and pray about ministry with a co-worker.

Pray immediately for the person. Ask God to give him or her a burden to be your prayer partner when you approach him or her. Ask God to give the person faith, wisdom, and ability to intercede for you.

Go talk with a potential prayer partner. You could have coffee or a meal together. Tell the person you've prayed and you're asking God to give you a prayer partner. Ask them to pray about being your partner. I would suggest you not press him or her for a decision the first time you talk. Rather, both of you should seek God's guidance in this relationship.

Plan how you will pray together. To make your prayer time with another more effective, use the following checklist to plan your time together:

- Decide a time you will meet.
- Agree how long you'll be together each time.
- Decide a place where you'll meet.
- Determine what resources you'll need, for example a prayer list, Bible study material, devotional reading, etc.
- Plan your schedule and how you'll use your time together.

Samuel thought intercessory prayer was so vital that he said, "God forbid that I should sin against the Lord in ceasing to pray for you" (1 Sa 12:23, KJV).

Suggested Reading: Exodus 17:5–16

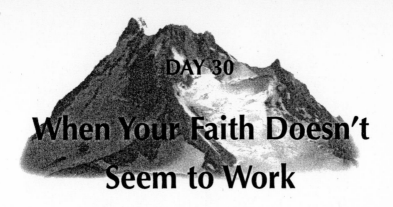

DAY 30

When Your Faith Doesn't
Seem to Work

"O Nebuchadnezzar . . . our God whom we serve is able to deliver us from the burning fiery furnace, and He will deliver us from your hand, O king. But if not, let it be known to you, O king, that we do not serve your gods, nor will we worship the gold image which you have set up."

(Da 3:16–18)

Sometimes you step out on faith, but things don't work out. Maybe you were convinced that something was God's will. You prayed by faith, but the answer didn't come. What happens when you don't get your answers to prayer?

Sometimes we humans are able to convince ourselves that God will do something, but we are wrong. Maybe we wanted something to happen for selfish reasons. James tells us, "You ask and do not receive, because you ask amiss, that you may spend it on your pleasures" (Jam 4:3).

God answers every prayer; He says yes, no, or wait. Sometimes God tells you no. Or He tells you to wait. What you want doesn't fit within His will because the timing is wrong.

Several times in my life God has told me no or wait. If I had not understood how to walk by faith, God's no could have discouraged me or made me think I was a failure. God's no could have damaged my faith. I don't want that to happen to you. When you don't get an answer to prayer, I don't want you to give up or lose your trust in God. Today's lesson explains how your faith can grow in the face of God's no.

The Wrong Time

In the early 1970s, I had a vision of taking *The Old Time Gospel Hour* into homes all across America for Bible study. I conceived a plan called America's Home Bible Class. I hired a born-again executive who had conceived a very successful marketing program with a secular company. He began putting together a program where I taught Bible lessons by tape cassette for use in the homes of my television viewers.

I wrote and we mailed a lesson outline for those in the classes, along with a cassette of the lesson. At the time, there were more than 110,000 Faith Partners who were sending ten dollars per month to support our television ministry. I thought these Faith Partners would feverishly gather their friends into their homes to study the Bible. I had a vision of 100,000 home classes.

At the time a church in South Korea reached more than 200,000 people weekly through 20,000 home cell groups. However, what worked in Korea didn't attract people in America. Americans were still committed to Sunday school classes. Most of my Faith Partners wanted to hear me preach over TV, not get their friends involved in small groups. I didn't correctly read the times and the home environment of Americans. No matter how much faith I exercised, and no matter how hard we worked, the program didn't happen at that time. We had to drop it. Now, twenty-five years later, these home groups are beginning to work, but back then they didn't.

Look at Hebrews 11:33–38 to see people whose faith didn't deliver them from problems. Some endured "mockings and scourgings, yes, and of chains and imprisonment" (v. 36). They had deep faith—faith to endure persecution—yet their faith didn't change their circumstances. The Bible was probably referring to Zechariah when it says, "They were stoned" (v. 37). It was probably referring to Isaiah when it says, "They were sawn in two" (v. 37), because most Bible scholars believe Isaiah was placed in a hollow tree and sawn in two. His faith didn't stop his martyrdom. Notice there were others whose faith didn't seem to provide for their basic needs; "They wandered in deserts and mountains, in dens and caves of the earth" (v. 38). Their faith didn't change their circumstances.

Maybe you've followed God and your faith has led you into a desert. Maybe you live in a symbolic cave. So what should you do? Make your desert a classroom to learn how to experience the presence of God in difficult circumstances. Make your cave a sanctuary where you can worship God. Because "the Father seeks worshippers" (Jo 4:24), when you worship in a cave, the Father comes to dwell with you and He makes your cave a sanctuary. Remember, God is glorified when you have faith in Him in spite of your circumstances.

Trusting God, Not Circumstances

Faith never judges God by circumstances. When you pray for money and it doesn't come, don't blame God. Don't ask "Why?" Maybe it's not God's time to give you money. Maybe God will answer a different way without money. Maybe you didn't understand God's will in the first place, and what you pray about is not what God wants to do. Faith has complete trust in God even when prayers are not answered. You don't trust in answered prayer, you trust in the Word of God.

You must believe God, even when you can't change your circumstances. Jeremiah had deep faith in God, but he was still thrown into a cesspool. In spite of his prayers, he suffered. Martyrs have had deep faith in God, even when flames were burning their bodies. Faith has deep trust in God in spite of the circumstances.

I've been in hospital rooms where cancer has struck a healthy body. The family has asked me, "Why did God do that?" That's a question I can't answer. Cancer is a medical condition with physical causes. We must never question God because of our circumstances. We must believe God, no matter what our circumstances.

I have had some family members of the sick ask me, "If God loved our mother, why would He have stricken her with cancer?" I also have heard, "If God loved our mother, why didn't He heal her?" Are these questions a lack of faith? No! These people haven't seen God's overall plan for the life of the sick person.

God wants us to have faith in Him in spite of our circumstances. God has promised us, "I will never leave you" (He 13:5), but He never promised us an easy time. God has said that we will sometimes "walk through the valley of the shadow of death" (Ps 23:4). He didn't promise to deliver us from difficulties, but He did promise to be with us in death's valley. Faith is not just getting out of death's valley; faith is accepting what He gives in the valley. Faith is fellowshipping with Him in shadows. Faith is being faithful unto death.

You must have a "but if not" attitude of faith. This is the attitude of the three young Hebrew men who would not bow down to Nebuchadnezzar's idol. King Nebuchadnezzar commanded everyone who wouldn't bow to the idol to be thrown into a fiery furnace. The three young men had deep faith in God. They refused to bow to an idol. They answered, "Our God whom we serve is able to deliver us from the burning fiery furnace, and He will deliver us from your hand, O king. *But if not*, let it be known to you, O king, that we do not serve your gods" (Da 3:17–18, italics added). By faith they wanted God to deliver them, and they believed He could. But if God didn't, by faith they were willing to become martyrs. *But if not*, they had faith to trust God in death.

Can you pray in faith, "Lord, heal, *but if not*, I accept the consequences"? Can you plan to construct a building and pray, "Lord, send us money, *but if not*, I will not build"?

Your outlook of faith must always triumph personally over your circumstances. Your faith may not change circumstances, but it can glorify God in difficult circumstances.

A pastor doesn't begin raising money by looking in the pockets of his people; he begins by looking to God. God is always the source. Your attitude of faith is more important than the success of your programs, or a healing of cancer, or an answer to prayer.

If your faith controls your life, then whether you get things is not important. Your faith determines your relationship with God, and that determines your outlook on life. When you have the right attitude, circumstances will not determine if you're a good Christian. Your outlook on your circumstances tells everyone you love Christ.

So, what's the bottom line? Faith always triumphs, whether or not circumstances change. If God wants to deliver you, He can do it. If God doesn't do it, God will go with you through "death's valley." Faith is not just receiving from God what you want; faith is the ability to accept what He gives and glorify Him in all circumstances.

Experiencing Faith

Review answers to prayer. Look back over your prayer list for the past thirty days. Check those items where you know God heard and answered. Don't let anything steal the confidence you got from God when He did something for you. "Being confident of this very thing, that He who has begun a good work in you will complete it until the day of Jesus Christ" (Ph 1:6).

Reflect. Try to put into words the feelings of confidence you received from an answer to prayer. Write a short one- or two-sentence summary of your inner assurance.

Honestly confess. Now I'm asking you to do something that's very hard to do. List one or two prayer requests to which God said no. Examine your inner motives. Were you praying for something that would reinforce your ego, or for a possession that you selfishly wanted? Maybe you were praying for something that would make you happy or comfortable. James says, "You ask and do not receive, because you ask amiss" and pray "that you may spend it on your pleasures" (Jam 4:3). Confess that you were praying for the wrong thing or with the wrong motive. Ask God to forgive you (1 Jo 1:9). Ask God to forgive the sin of your heart (Lk 5:21–24).

Thank God for times He says no. I knew a boy in Bible college who had trouble getting dates with girls. When a girl went out with him, he fell madly in love with each one and was sure at the time God wanted him to marry her. Today, he's very successful in ministry and thanks God that his prayers for all those girls were not answered yes. Sometimes our faith is strengthened when we look back at the prayers God answered no.

If God has said no to any of your prayers, look back and thank God. It'll strengthen your faith.

Suggested Reading: Daniel 3

Today Counts[1]

> "Therefore we also, since we are surrounded by so great a cloud of witnesses, let us lay aside every weight, and the sin which so easily ensnares us, and let us run with endurance the race that is set before us, looking unto Jesus, the author and finisher of our faith."
>
> (He 12:1–2)

We have spent one month discussing faith. I want to end by focusing your life on Jesus. As the above verse states, He is the "finisher of our faith." That means you live each day by keeping your eyes on Him. Jesus is at the finish line waiting for you, and you live by faith because He is your God.

But Jesus helps you each day as you race toward the finish line. He lives within your heart and motivates you daily to do your best. He helps you finish your *faith journey*.

To live by faith each day you should review your goal in life, which is your *faith purpose* (Day 5). My good friend Rick Warren has written an outstanding book, *The Purpose Driven Life*, that encourages believers to continually focus on the purpose God has for each of us.

Also, when you live by faith, you should follow a daily *life plan* (Day 9). This is the road map that you've developed by which you direct your daily activities.

Living by faith is managing your life by purpose, and each day doing the plans that God wants you to do. However, proper management means having the proper attitude toward yesterday, tomorrow, and today. Many people live in the past; yesterday is the most important day of their lives. I jokingly say they are dragged kicking and screaming into a future where they are not prepared to live. Those who constantly live in yesterday accomplish little for God.

Other people live primarily in the future. They give so much time thinking and planning for the future that they forget about the present. Many of these people "live" in a future that never arrives. So these people also do little for God.

When we live by faith, we live each day—one day at a time. We do what we have to do and we do it with all our might (Col 3:23). We make each day count. That's God's way to live by faith. Is that the way you are living?

Yesterday, Tomorrow, and Today

Do you know what you get from the three aspects of time: the past, present, and future? Tomorrow is the future that gives you energy to make plans for what you're going to do. You'll get excited and you'll sacrifice to reach your dreams. By faith you must plan for your tomorrows and work out your *life purpose*.

The past is foundational to all you are and do. By faith you must learn from your past, build upon your past, and do better than you did in the past. You can't undo your past, and you can't go back to redo your history. Thank God for who you are and what He has made of you. Thank God for your weaknesses and your strengths. You can't exercise spiritual gifts you don't have, any more than you can come back from where you've never been. Take advantage of your past, but don't live there. Those living in the past are filled with regrets. They have little energy to face the future because the past won't return, and they are not equipping themselves for the future.

Today is the most important day in your life. Today counts. Today you can change things you don't like in your life. Today you can pray for your dreams and make *life plans* to accomplish your *life purpose*. Today is a new opportunity to do all the things you've dreamed of in the past.

When I pillow my head each evening, I don't rejoice in what I accomplished in the past day. I don't recount the money I've raised for Liberty University®, nor do I revisit in my mind the buildings I've built, or the large exciting events I've been a part of. No! That's history and I can't do anything about them. When I go to bed at night, I think of new and more exciting challenges . . . bigger and better buildings to be built . . . and new church events that will bring glory to God. The future is where we'll all live, so let's plan for it, and work for it, and pray for it.

Your prayer list should be filled with things you want to do for God. Don't be a "history-lover" who yearns for the good ol' days and wants to return to live in "horse and buggy" days. Past revivals were great, but pray and plan for the greatest revival you've ever seen. Charles Spurgeon, John Wesley, and Martin Luther did great things for God in the past, but let's plan to do greater things in the future.

Remember, we serve a God who can do the impossible, "For with God nothing will be impossible" (Lk 1:37). People laugh when I tell them, "I'm too busy to die." They also laugh when I say I have a twenty-year plan—as I write I'm 71 years old—but I've got a lot of things I want to do for God before I die. And when I go home to see my Lord, I'll be in the driver's seat looking down the road at the future. I'll not be an old man rocking on the front porch surveying all my past accomplishments.

Making the Most of Today

The past is foundational and the future gives us energy. What about today? Today counts! It doesn't count for just a little, it counts for everything. Today needs all your attention . . . all your energy . . . all your prayers and work. Because if you don't make today all it can be, then you're ignoring the lessons and foundation of the past. If you don't make today count, then the dreams of to-morrow will never materialize.

You must work as hard as you can today, because today counts! You must plan your activities, discipline your time, and follow up on details because today counts. If you don't make every day the best that it can be, then all of your visions and goals of the future are only daydreams. I use the term *daydreams* here in a negative context, describing an irresponsible person who only *wishes* things would get better. By faith you must have a *life purpose* that makes you *work* to accomplish all God has for you.

So you must have faith to harness all three time elements—past, present, and future. By faith you read the past accomplishments of heroes in Hebrews 11 and determine to follow their example. By faith you examine your past life—thanking God for victories and learning from where you failed. By faith you determine to do it better or do it differently. By faith you determine to climb higher in the future.

You follow your examples of faith: "These all died in faith, not having received the promises, but having seen them afar off were assured of them, embraced them and confessed that they were strangers and pilgrims on the earth" (He 11:13).

It takes faith to plan your future. Look at Abraham: "He waited for the city . . . whose builder and maker is God" (He 11:10). Abraham "by faith" endured desert-living with no house and no garden, nor did he own any property. Abraham was future-oriented because He believed God would keep His promise to give him the Promised Land.

You too must plan your future based on the promises of God. The life of faith is looking to Jesus, even though you face difficulties. "Let us run with endurance the race that is set before us, looking unto Jesus, the author and finisher of our faith" (He 12:1–2).

But the person of faith should never get so hung up on the past or future that he forgets today. Today is more important than the other two elements of time. "By faith Abraham obeyed . . . and he went out . . ." (He 11:8). Abraham didn't wait for the good ol' days to come back. Abraham didn't just wait for future promises to materialize. "One day" Abraham obeyed and left home to go to the Promised Land. That "one day" later became the *yesterday* upon which his faith was founded. Abraham acted "one day" because of the *future* day he dreamed of happening. That "one day" became the day that changed his life. That "one day" happened when Abraham realized, "Today counts!"

Since today counts, what projects can you do for God now? Since today counts, what changes will you make in your life for God now?

Jesus said, "Follow Me" (Mk 1:17), but He added, "and I will make you become fishers of men." Jesus was asking for an instantaneous response. He was not asking for the disciples to think about the past and their accomplishments. He was not asking for them to make plans for future activity. On that "one day," Jesus asked the disciples to follow Him. That day counted for eternity because "they left . . . and followed Him" (v. 20).

Today counts in your life and mine. Jesus calls us to follow Him today. Will you make today the "one day" that changes your life? Will you follow Jesus today?

By the time you read this, I may be in heaven with Jesus, or I could still be alive. If God grants me more years, I want to win more battles, construct more buildings for Liberty University®, recruit more students, and plant more churches. My greatest challenge will always be tomorrow, so I'll have to work hard to make each "today count" so I'll have more victories in the coming "tomorrows."

Experiencing Faith

Obviously God will give you many more assignments in your life, but this is the final one that I'll give you in this book.

Review your life purpose. The most important thing in your life from this day forward is to live daily by your *life purpose*. Repeat it often and let it give direction to your life.

Keep your life plan updated. This is the road map that directs daily steps. When the geography changes, you'll have to update your map. There will be reversals in life; a bridge may collapse or a road be closed, so you'll need new road maps. For reasons you don't know now, your occupation may change; someone close may die and your *life plan* may have depended on him or her. Don't change your *life purpose,* but you may need to get there by another path. You'll have to update your *life plan.*

Keep your commitments. Earlier you committed yourself to meeting God daily to talk to Him in prayer and read His Word. Don't let anything get between you and God.

Be active. Continue to serve the Lord. Don't just work because you *have* to; serve the Lord from a grateful heart. Do it because you *want* to.

Make today the best. You may never have another opportunity to do your best for God, so make today count! Determine now to give your best to this day in everything you do.

Rely on His strength. As you live for God this day, He will help you in ways you've never before realized. When you do things for God that you've never done before, you'll get help from Him that you never experienced. "As your days, so shall your strength [be]" (De 33:25).

Suggested Reading: Hebrews 11:1–12:2

Notes

Day 3

1. "Help in Time of Need," adapted from The Gideons International website, <http://www.gideons.org> (accessed 30 November 2004).

Day 4

1. Otis and Jim are still in Thomas Road Baptist Church as I write this book.
2. Charlotte Elliott, *Just As I Am*, 1841.

Day 7

1. Another good source is Brother Lawrence, *The Practice of the Presence of God: With Spiritual Maxims* (Grand Rapids, Mich.: Fleming Revell, Reprint edition, 1999).

Day 9

1. St. Augustine, "Brainy Quote," <http://www.brainyquote.com/quotes/quotes/s/saintaugus165165.html> (accessed 11 January 2005).

Day 10

1. Alfred Lord Tennyson, "The Passing of Arthur," *The Camelot Project at the University of Rochester*, <http://www.lib.rochester.edu/camelot/idyl-pas.htm> (accessed 23 April 2004).
2. Rick Warren, *The Purpose-Driven Church* (Grand Rapids, Mich.: Zondervan, 1995), 99.

Day 18

1. Watchman Nee, *The Normal Christian Life* (Ft. Washington, Pa.: Christian Literature Crusade, 1957; reprint Lynchburg, VA: The Old Time Gospel Hour, special edition, 1973), 101.

Day 31

1. The ideas for this chapter come from a book by my good friend, John Maxwell, *Today Matters* (New York: Little, Brown and Company, 2004).

APPENDIX

Daily Scripture Reading Plan

Calendar for Daily Reading of Scriptures

JANUARY

DATE	MORNING		EVENING		DATE	MORNING		EVENING	
1	Ge	1, 2, 3	Ma	1	17	Ge	41, 42	Ma	12: 1–23
2	Ge	4, 5, 6	Ma	2	18	Ge	43, 44, 45	Ma	12:24–50
3	Ge	7, 8, 9	Ma	3	19	Ge	46, 47, 48	Ma	13: 1–30
4	Ge	10, 11, 12	Ma	4	20	Ge	49, 50	Ma	13:31–58
5	Ge	13, 14, 15	Ma	5: 1–26	21	Ex	1, 2, 3	Ma	14: 1–21
6	Ge	16, 17	Ma	5:27–48	22	Ex	4, 5, 6	Ma	14:22–36
7	Ge	18, 19	Ma	6: 1–18	23	Ex	7, 8	Ma	15: 1–20
8	Ge	20, 21, 22	Ma	6:19–34	24	Ex	9, 10, 11	Ma	15:21–39
9	Ge	23, 24	Ma	7	25	Ex	12, 13	Ma	16
10	Ge	25, 26	Ma	8: 1–17	26	Ex	14, 15	Ma	17
11	Ge	27, 28	Ma	8:18–34	27	Ex	16, 17, 18	Ma	18: 1–20
12	Ge	29, 30	Ma	9: 1–17	28	Ex	19, 20	Ma	18:21–35
13	Ge	31, 32	Ma	9:18–38	29	Ex	21, 22	Ma	19
14	Ge	33, 34, 35	Ma	10: 1–20	30	Ex	23, 24	Ma	20: 1–16
15	Ge	36, 37, 38	Ma	10:21–42	31	Ex	25, 26	Ma	20:17–34
16	Ge	39, 40	Ma	11					

FEBRUARY

DATE	MORNING		EVENING		DATE	MORNING		EVENING	
1	Ex	27, 28	Ma	21: 1–22	16	Le	19, 20	Ma	27:51–66
2	Ex	29, 30	Ma	21:23–46	17	Le	21, 22	Ma	28
3	Ex	31, 32, 33	Ma	22: 1–22	18	Le	23, 24	Mk	1: 1–22
4	Ex	34, 35	Ma	22:23–46	19	Le	25	Mk	1:23–45
5	Ex	36, 37, 38	Ma	23: 1–22	20	Le	26, 27	Mk	2
6	Ex	39, 40	Ma	23:23–39	21	Nu	1, 2	Mk	3: 1–19
7	Le	1, 2, 3	Ma	24: 1–28	22	Nu	3, 4	Mk	3:20–35
8	Le	4, 5	Ma	24:29–51	23	Nu	5, 6	Mk	4: 1–20
9	Le	6, 7	Ma	25: 1–30	24	Nu	7, 8	Mk	4:21–41
10	Le	8, 9, 10	Ma	25:31–46	25	Nu	9, 10, 11	Mk	5: 1–20
11	Le	11, 12	Ma	26: 1–25	26	Nu	12, 13, 14	Mk	5:21–43
12	Le	13	Ma	26:26–50	27	Nu	15, 16	Mk	6: 1–29
13	Le	14	Ma	26:51–75	28	Nu	17, 18, 19	Mk	6:30–56
14	Le	15, 16	Ma	27: 1–26	29	Nu	20, 21, 22	Mk	7: 1–13
15	Le	17, 18	Ma	27:27–50					

Note—When February has only twenty-eight days, read the portion for the 29th with that for the 28th.

MARCH

DATE	MORNING		EVENING		DATE	MORNING		EVENING	
1	Nu	23, 24, 25	Mk	7:14–37	17	De	30, 31	Mk	15: 1–25
2	Nu	26, 27	Mk	8: 1–21	18	De	32, 33, 34	Mk	15:26–47
3	Nu	28, 29, 30	Mk	8:22–38	19	Jos	1, 2, 3	Mk	16
4	Nu	31, 32, 33	Mk	9: 1–29	20	Jos	4, 5, 6	Lk	1: 1–20
5	Nu	34, 35, 36	Mk	9:30–50	21	Jos	7, 8, 9	Lk	1:21–38
6	De	1, 2	Mk	10: 1–31	22	Jos	10, 11, 12	Lk	1:39–56
7	De	3, 4	Mk	10:32–52	23	Jos	13, 14, 15	Lk	1:57–80
8	De	5, 6, 7	Mk	11: 1–18	24	Jos	16, 17, 18	Lk	2: 1–24
9	De	8, 9, 10	Mk	11:19–33	25	Jos	19, 20, 21	Lk	2:25–52
10	De	11, 12, 13	Mk	12: 1–27	26	Jos	22, 23, 24	Lk	3
11	De	14, 15, 16	Mk	12:28–44	27	Ju	1, 2, 3	Lk	4: 1–30
12	De	17, 18, 19	Mk	13: 1–20	28	Ju	4, 5, 6	Lk	4:31–44
13	De	20, 21, 22	Mk	13:21–37	29	Ju	7, 8	Lk	5: 1–16
14	De	23, 24, 25	Mk	14: 1–26	30	Ju	9, 10	Lk	5:17–39
15	De	26, 27	Mk	14:27–53	31	Ju	11, 12	Lk	6: 1–26
16	De	28, 29	Mk	14:54–72					

Calendar for Daily Reading of Scriptures

APRIL

DATE	MORNING	EVENING	DATE	MORNING	EVENING
1	Ju 13, 14, 15	Lk 6:27–49	16	1 Sa 30, 31	Lk 13:23–35
2	Ju 16, 17, 18	Lk 7: 1–30	17	2 Sa 1, 2	Lk 14: 1–24
3	Ju 19, 20, 21	Lk 7:31–50	18	2 Sa 3, 4, 5	Lk 14:25–35
4	Ru 1, 2, 3, 4	Lk 8: 1–25	19	2 Sa 6, 7, 8	Lk 15: 1–10
5	1 Sa 1, 2, 3	Lk 8:26–56	20	2 Sa 9, 10, 11	Lk 15:11–32
6	1 Sa 4, 5, 6	Lk 9: 1–17	21	2 Sa 12, 13	Lk 16
7	1 Sa 7, 8, 9	Lk 9:18–36	22	2 Sa 14, 15	Lk 17: 1–19
8	1 Sa 10, 11, 12	Lk 9:37–62	23	2 Sa 16, 17, 18	Lk 17:20–37
9	1 Sa 13, 14	Lk 10: 1–24	24	2 Sa 19, 20	Lk 18: 1–23
10	1 Sa 15, 16	Lk 10:25–42	25	2 Sa 21, 22	Lk 18:24–43
11	1 Sa 17, 18	Lk 11: 1–28	26	2 Sa 23, 24	Lk 19: 1–27
12	1 Sa 19, 20, 21	Lk 11:29–54	27	1 Ki 1, 2	Lk 19:28–48
13	1 Sa 22, 23, 24	Lk 12: 1–31	28	1 Ki 3, 4, 5	Lk 20: 1–26
14	1 Sa 25, 26	Lk 12:32–59	29	1 Ki 6, 7	Lk 20:27–47
15	1 Sa 27, 28, 29	Lk 13: 1–22	30	1 Ki 8, 9	Lk 21: 1–19

MAY

DATE	MORNING	EVENING	DATE	MORNING	EVENING
1	1 Ki 10, 11	Lk 21:20–38	17	1 Ch 1, 2, 3	Jo 5:25–47
2	1 Ki 12, 13	Lk 22: 1–20	18	1 Ch 4, 5, 6	Jo 6: 1–21
3	1 Ki 14, 15	Lk 22:21–46	19	1 Ch 7, 8, 9	Jo 6:22–44
4	1 Ki 16, 17, 18	Lk 22:47–71	20	1 Ch 10, 11, 12	Jo 6:45–71
5	1 Ki 19, 20	Lk 23: 1–25	21	1 Ch 13, 14, 15	Jo 7: 1–27
6	1 Ki 21, 22	Lk 23:26–56	22	1 Ch 16, 17, 18	Jo 7:28–53
7	2 Ki 1, 2, 3	Lk 24: 1–35	23	1 Ch 19, 20, 21	Jo 8: 1–27
8	2 Ki 4, 5, 6	Lk 24:36–53	24	1 Ch 22, 23, 24	Jo 8:28–59
9	2 Ki 7, 8, 9	Jo 1: 1–28	25	1 Ch 25, 26, 27	Jo 9: 1–23
10	2 Ki 10, 11, 12	Jo 1:29–51	26	1 Ch 28, 29	Jo 9:24–41
11	2 Ki 13, 14	Jo 2	27	2 Ch 1, 2, 3	Jo 10: 1–23
12	2 Ki 15, 16	Jo 3: 1–18	28	2 Ch 4, 5, 6	Jo 10:24–42
13	2 Ki 17, 18	Jo 3:19–36	29	2 Ch 7, 8, 9	Jo 11: 1–29
14	2 Ki 19, 20, 21	Jo 4: 1–30	30	2 Ch 10, 11, 12	Jo 11:30–57
15	2 Ki 22, 23	Jo 4:31–54	31	2 Ch 13, 14	Jo 12: 1–26
16	2 Ki 24, 25	Jo 5: 1–24			

JUNE

DATE	MORNING	EVENING	DATE	MORNING	EVENING
1	2 Ch 15, 16	Jo 12:27–50	16	Ne 4, 5, 6	Ac 2:22–47
2	2 Ch 17, 18	Jo 13: 1–20	17	Ne 7, 8, 9	Ac 3
3	2 Ch 19, 20	Jo 13:21–38	18	Ne 10, 11	Ac 4: 1–22
4	2 Ch 21, 22	Jo 14	19	Ne 12, 13	Ac 4:23–37
5	2 Ch 23, 24	Jo 15	20	Es 1, 2	Ac 5: 1–21
6	2 Ch 25, 26, 27	Jo 16	21	Es 3, 4, 5	Ac 5:22–42
7	2 Ch 28, 29	Jo 17	22	Es 6, 7, 8	Ac 6
8	2 Ch 30, 31	Jo 18: 1–18	23	Es 9, 10	Ac 7: 1–21
9	2 Ch 32, 33	Jo 18:19–40	24	Job 1, 2	Ac 7:22–43
10	2 Ch 34, 35, 36	Jo 19: 1–22	25	Job 3, 4	Ac 7:44–60
11	Ez 1, 2	Jo 19:23–42	26	Job 5, 6, 7	Ac 8: 1–25
12	Ez 3, 4, 5	Jo 20	27	Job 8, 9, 10	Ac 8:26–40
13	Ez 6, 7, 8	Jo 21	28	Job 11, 12, 13	Ac 9: 1–21
14	Ez 9, 10	Ac 1	29	Job 14, 15, 16	Ac 9:22–43
15	Ne 1, 2, 3	Ac 2: 1–21	30	Job 17, 18, 19	Ac 10: 1–23

Calendar for Daily Reading of Scriptures

JULY

DATE	MORNING			EVENING		DATE	MORNING			EVENING	
1	Job	20,	21	Ac	10:24–48	17	Ps	18,	19	Ac	20:17–38
2	Job	22,	23, 24	Ac	11	18	Ps	20,	21, 22	Ac	21: 1–17
3	Job	25,	26, 27	Ac	12	19	Ps	23,	24, 25	Ac	21:18–40
4	Job	28,	29	Ac	13: 1–25	20	Ps	26,	27, 28	Ac	22
5	Job	30,	31	Ac	13:26–52	21	Ps	29,	30	Ac	23: 1–15
6	Job	32,	33	Ac	14	22	Ps	31,	32	Ac	23:16–35
7	Job	34,	35	Ac	15: 1–21	23	Ps	33,	34	Ac	24
8	Job	36,	37	Ac	15:22–41	24	Ps	35,	36	Ac	25
9	Job	38,	39, 40	Ac	16: 1–21	25	Ps	37,	38, 39	Ac	26
10	Job	41,	42	Ac	16:22–40	26	Ps	40,	41, 42	Ac	27: 1–26
11	Ps	1,	2, 3	Ac	17: 1–15	27	Ps	43,	44, 45	Ac	27:27–44
12	Ps	4,	5, 6	Ac	17:16–34	28	Ps	46,	47, 48	Ac	28
13	Ps	7,	8, 9	Ac	18	29	Ps	49,	50	Ro	1
14	Ps	10,	11, 12	Ac	19: 1–20	30	Ps	51,	52, 53	Ro	2
15	Ps	13,	14, 15	Ac	19:21–41	31	Ps	54,	55, 56	Ro	3
16	Ps	16,	17	Ac	20: 1–16						

AUGUST

DATE	MORNING			EVENING		DATE	MORNING			EVENING	
1	Ps	57,	58, 59	Ro	4	17	Ps	97,	98, 99	Ro	16
2	Ps	60,	61, 62	Ro	5	18	Ps	100,	101, 102	1 Co	1
3	Ps	63,	64, 65	Ro	6	19	Ps	103,	104	1 Co	2
4	Ps	66,	67	Ro	7	20	Ps	105,	106	1 Co	3
5	Ps	68,	69	Ro	8: 1–21	21	Ps	107,	108, 109	1 Co	4
6	Ps	70,	71	Ro	8:22–39	22	Ps	110,	111, 112	1 Co	5
7	Ps	72,	73	Ro	9: 1–15	23	Ps	113,	114, 115	1 Co	6
8	Ps	74,	75, 76	Ro	9:16–33	24	Ps	116,	117, 118	1 Co	7: 1–19
9	Ps	77,	78	Ro	10	25	Ps	119:	1–88	1 Co	7:20–40
10	Ps	79,	80	Ro	11: 1–18	26	Ps	119:	89–176	1 Co	8
11	Ps	81,	82, 83	Ro	11:19–36	27	Ps	120,	121, 122	1 Co	9
12	Ps	84,	85, 86	Ro	12	28	Ps	123,	124, 125	1 Co	10: 1–18
13	Ps	87,	88	Ro	13	29	Ps	126,	127, 128	1 Co	10:19–33
14	Ps	89,	90	Ro	14	30	Ps	129,	130, 131	1 Co	11: 1–16
15	Ps	91,	92, 93	Ro	15: 1–13	31	Ps	132,	133, 134	1 Co	11:17–34
16	Ps	94,	95, 96	Ro	15:14–33						

SEPTEMBER

DATE	MORNING			EVENING		DATE	MORNING			EVENING	
1	Ps	135,	136	1 Co	12	16	Pr	25,	26	2 Co	9
2	Ps	137,	138, 139	1 Co	13	17	Pr	27,	28, 29	2 Co	10
3	Ps	140,	141, 142	1 Co	14: 1–20	18	Pr	30,	31	2 Co	11: 1–15
4	Ps	143,	144, 145	1 Co	14:21–40	19	Ec	1,	2, 3	2 Co	11:16–33
5	Ps	146,	147	1 Co	15: 1–28	20	Ec	4,	5, 6	2 Co	12
6	Ps	148,	149, 150	1 Co	15:29–58	21	Ec	7,	8, 9	2 Co	13
7	Pr	1,	2	1 Co	16	22	Ec	10,	11, 12	Ga	1
8	Pr	3,	4, 5	2 Co	1	23	Song	1,	2, 3	Ga	2
9	Pr	6,	7	2 Co	2	24	Song	4,	5	Ga	3
10	Pr	8,	9	2 Co	3	25	Song	6,	7, 8	Ga	4
11	Pr	10,	11, 12	2 Co	4	26	Is	1,	2	Ga	5
12	Pr	13,	14, 15	2 Co	5	27	Is	3,	4	Ga	6
13	Pr	16,	17, 18	2 Co	6	28	Is	5,	6	Ep	1
14	Pr	19,	20, 21	2 Co	7	29	Is	7,	8	Ep	2
15	Pr	22,	23, 24	2 Co	8	30	Is	9,	10	Ep	3

Calendar for Daily Reading of Scriptures

OCTOBER

DATE	MORNING	EVENING	DATE	MORNING	EVENING
1	Is 11, 12, 13	Ep 4	17	Is 50, 51, 52	1 Th 5
2	Is 14, 15, 16	Ep 5: 1–16	18	Is 53, 54, 55	2 Th 1
3	Is 17, 18, 19	Ep 5:17–33	19	Is 56, 57, 58	2 Th 2
4	Is 20, 21, 22	Ep 6	20	Is 59, 60, 61	2 Th 3
5	Is 23, 24, 25	Ph 1	21	Is 62, 63, 64	1 Ti 1
6	Is 26, 27	Ph 2	22	Is 65, 66	1 Ti 2
7	Is 28, 29	Ph 3	23	Je 1, 2	1 Ti 3
8	Is 30, 31	Ph 4	24	Je 3, 4, 5	1 Ti 4
9	Is 32, 33	Col 1	25	Je 6, 7, 8	1 Ti 5
10	Is 34, 35, 36	Col 2	26	Je 9, 10, 11	1 Ti 6
11	Is 37, 38	Col 3	27	Je 12, 13, 14	2 Ti 1
12	Is 39, 40	Col 4	28	Je 15, 16, 17	2 Ti 2
13	Is 41, 42	1 Th 1	29	Je 18, 19	2 Ti 3
14	Is 43, 44	1 Th 2	30	Je 20, 21	2 Ti 4
15	Is 45, 46	1 Th 3	31	Je 22, 23	Tit 1
16	Is 47, 48, 49	1 Th 4			

NOVEMBER

DATE	MORNING	EVENING	DATE	MORNING	EVENING
1	Je 24, 25, 26	Tit 2	16	Eze 3, 4	He 11:20–40
2	Je 27, 28, 29	Tit 3	17	Eze 5, 6, 7	He 12
3	Je 30, 31	Phile	18	Eze 8, 9, 10	He 13
4	Je 32, 33	He 1	19	Eze 11, 12, 13	Jam 1
5	Je 34, 35, 36	He 2	20	Eze 14, 15	Jam 2
6	Je 37, 38, 39	He 3	21	Eze 16, 17	Jam 3
7	Je 40, 41, 42	He 4	22	Eze 18, 19	Jam 4
8	Je 43, 44, 45	He 5	23	Eze 20, 21	Jam 5
9	Je 46, 47	He 6	24	Eze 22, 23	1 Pe 1
10	Je 48, 49	He 7	25	Eze 24, 25, 26	1 Pe 2
11	Je 50	He 8	26	Eze 27, 28, 29	1 Pe 3
12	Je 51, 52	He 9	27	Eze 30, 31, 32	1 Pe 4
13	La 1, 2	He 10: 1–18	28	Eze 33, 34	1 Pe 5
14	La 3, 4, 5	He 10:19–39	29	Eze 35, 36	2 Pe 1
15	Eze 1, 2	He 11: 1–19	30	Eze 37, 38, 39	2 Pe 2

DECEMBER

DATE	MORNING	EVENING	DATE	MORNING	EVENING
1	Eze 40, 41	2 Pe 3	17	Am 7, 8, 9	Re 8
2	Eze 42, 43, 44	1 Jo 1	18	Ob	Re 9
3	Eze 45, 46	1 Jo 2	19	Jon 1, 2, 3, 4	Re 10
4	Eze 47, 48	1 Jo 3	20	Mi 1, 2, 3	Re 11
5	Da 1, 2	1 Jo 4	21	Mi 4, 5	Re 12
6	Da 3, 4	1 Jo 5	22	Mi 6, 7	Re 13
7	Da 5, 6, 7	2 Jo	23	Na 1, 2, 3	Re 14
8	Da 8, 9, 10	3 Jo	24	Hab 1, 2, 3	Re 15
9	Da 11, 12	Jude	25	Zep 1, 2, 3	Re 16
10	Ho 1, 2, 3, 4	Re 1	26	Hag 1, 2	Re 17
11	Ho 5, 6, 7, 8	Re 2	27	Ze 1, 2, 3, 4	Re 18
12	Ho 9, 10, 11	Re 3	28	Ze 5, 6, 7, 8	Re 19
13	Ho 12, 13, 14	Re 4	29	Ze 9, 10, 11, 12	Re 20
14	Joel 1, 2, 3	Re 5	30	Ze 13, 14	Re 21
15	Am 1, 2, 3	Re 6	31	Mal 1, 2, 3, 4	Re 22
16	Am 4, 5, 6	Re 7			

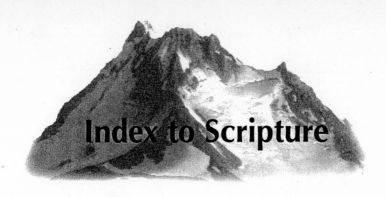

Index to Scripture

225

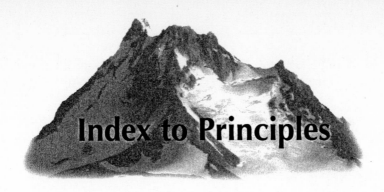

Index to Principles